THY KI CC

Volume 1
Living a Kingdom Lifestyle

Beryl Moore

SERVING THE KING

SOVEREIGN MINISTRIES
BERYL MOORE

Sovereign Ministries
www.sovereignministries.co.uk

ISBN: 978-1-908154-46-0

A catalogue record for this book is available from the British Library

Cover design by Esther Kotecha, EKDesign
Typeset by Avocet Typeset, Bideford, Devon, EX39 2BP
Printed and bound in the UK

TABLE OF CONTENTS

Contents

Contents

Section 3: Living from a higher place   **219**

Contents

DEDICATION

I dedicate this book to the Holy Spirit by whose power the prophets of old were carried along as, they *spake to the people of the things of God'* (2 Peter 1:21 KJV) and in so doing enabled them to hear

His Majesty

FOREWORD

Beryl's message is simple and can be described in one word. That word is 'higher'. Like an instructor in the high jump Beryl carefully raises the bar incrementally, just enough so that almost without realising it the reader is being raised up with Jesus Christ to new heights and a new vision of what is possible for their life. For those wanting to grow in faith, using the teaching in this book is a transformative experience. The expectation is growth and maturity in Christ. The aim is the realisation of a Kingdom vision and a Kingdom lifestyle governed by the Holy Spirit.

In this book the core teaching of Jesus is uncovered step-by-step, showing the reader not only what to do but how to do it. This is a practical course of instruction served in digestible portions.

'Thy Kingdom Come' should come with a health warning. Properly applied it will seriously damage your complacency and could even change the course of your life. You have been warned.

Rev. Doctor Christopher Noble
Kent, United Kingdom

PREFACE

The year 1991, the time, eight o'clock in the evening: no one had arrived.

The invitation had been to attend my first teaching on the subject of the Sermon on the Mount. I breathed a sigh of relief. I had never done this before and it looked as though I wasn't going to do it now.

Hearing the sound of doors slamming I glanced out of the window to see five or six cars and people spilling out. I was not off the hook. As they arrived, I took a deep breath and with some trepidation began to teach: "You have heard it said, but I say to you'.

Now, I take another very deep breath in great trepidation, knowing I handle the precious word of God Himself, the All Mighty One, and commit to print what He has revealed over the intervening years. This is not a definitive or finished work, as any author will tell you the moment you lay down your pen, more thoughts come. But weak as it is, as you travel with me through it and therefore through my own journey of discovery, my prayer is that you will come to know Him in a way you did not know Him before. He really is life's summum bonum; life's fulness. Abundance. All and everything you need or want forever; in this life and the next.

He will always be to you exactly what you need most.

God bless you.

Beryl
October 2019

INTRODUCTION

Central to every Bible study must be the majesty and supremacy of the Lord Jesus Christ. If it does not point to Him as the Alpha and the Omega it is time wasted; empty spiritual calories. He is our Lodestar, the centre of the Universe, Creator and Sustainer of all things. You are His people, His nation, His bride, and it is to you that these messages are directed. You have a destiny. That destiny is to reign and rule with Him for eternity. Your time here is but preparation for that task. My aim, in opening up the Sermon on the Mount is that you will be fully equipped to step into that role of co-regent when Jesus comes for you – that you may understand and be ready to live in the culture of heaven.

'The messenger of God', the Quakers used to say, must *'speak to the condition of his hearers.'* He or she *must* speak the language of his or her generation if they are to be heard.

The primary role of a prophet in the earth is to teach God's people to hear what the Spirit is saying to the churches, and when they hear to respond. My prayer is this book will *'speak to your condition'* and cause you to respond. That it will open the ears of those who were deaf, the eyes of those who were blind, and loosen the tongue of the dumb in adoration and worship of the Author of it, our Coming King and Bridegroom, His Majesty, the Lord Jesus Christ.

Beryl Moore

To Him I humbly dedicate this work: His Majesty, whom I love with all my heart, soul, and mind, and serve with all my strength; before whom I bow, to whom all praise honour and glory is due, world without end. Amen.

> *'The Chief end of man is to glorify God*
> *and enjoy Him forever.'*
> *Westminster Shorter Catechism*

Section 1

A long habit…

'A long habit of not thinking a thing wrong, gives it a superficial appearance of being right, and raises at first a formidable outcry in defense of custom. But tumult soon subsides. Time makes more converts than reason.'

Thomas Paine, 'Common Sense' Pennsylvania,
February 14, 1776, Public domain.

1
Introduction

A long habit of not thinking a thing wrong, gives it a superficial appearance of being right, and raises at first a formidable outcry in defence of custom. But tumult soon subsides. Time makes more converts than reason' [1]

This book is about the King, His Kingdom and the church.

Jesus was a revolutionary; He turned the world upside down when He came preaching the Kingdom.

His Kingdom is eternal and internal; it is a theocracy and it is about government.

In Matthew 6:33 we are told to seek it first. The government of the King in our lives.

This Kingdom is organic; it grows from a seed, the good seed planted in us at the rebirth.

The Kingdom comes down to us and into us in order that we may ascend to where it is. That we may live an ascended lifestyle.

The Kingdom comes to elevate us to another place from which to live. From heaven to earth, not the other way around.

The Kingdom is within us.

Jesus taught the nature of this Kingdom and the terms of membership in Matthew chapters 5,6 and 7 and Luke 22:24-27.

This Kingdom brings forth fruit: 30, 60 and 100-fold.

It has a manifesto and rules of engagement.

Unless we become as little children, we cannot enter it; that is we become like children, mouldable, correctable, and teachable.

We may need to unlearn all we have previously thought we know about it, as it comes to displace and take over.

The purpose of the battle is victory and the purpose of victory is occupation.

The Kingdom of heaven will enlighten us, but it will, at times, be inconvenient.

Being inconveniently enlightened means that when truth comes it does not tell us what we want to hear, nor does it agree with what we were sure were the facts. It presents us with a choice between loving our present darkness and loving the truth, in the Person of the Lord Jesus Christ.

If we really, really want to know the truth we are willing to develop the skill of repentance, changing our mind.

Christ discipled the twelve, incrementally teaching them what it meant to act against themselves. He taught them and us both by example and by biblical precept.

This teaching will not minister to your fallen nature, but if you embrace it, it will cause you to grow into maturity both emotionally and spiritually.

There is another King and His kingdom is the Kingdom of Love. His subjects are required to learn this new way of living, to understand the culture. This is called being a disciple.

When the King comes He comes to take over not to take sides. His Kingdom is within you.

The Kingdom of heaven is eternal, internal, divine and unshakeable. It is now and not yet. It is likened to a tree that can grow big enough for birds to make their nests.

The King of the Kingdom is the King of Love and the law of the Kingdom is Love.

The Kingdom manifesto is the Sermon on the Mount.

The law is that of responding in the opposite spirit. Turning the other cheek. Going the extra mile.

It is the Kingdom where Love is the key that opens every door, where our rule of life becomes: *'No matter what any* man does to me I will never seek anything but his highest good.'

'If a man loves God, he will not have any problem loving others' said Henry Drummond, in his little book 'The Greatest thing in the world'[2]

> "If you love God, you will unconsciously fulfil the whole law. You would not kill one you loved; you would not steal from him; you would not speak evil of him; you would have no need to require reverence for parents – if you loved: nor would you covet what anyone had, rather you would take pleasure that they had these things; to be told to keep the Sabbath unto God would be a pleasure, not a chore, if you loved Him..." (paraphrase)

Christ's one law for the Christian life is love. (Romans 13:8-14).

The *royal* law. Astonishing, amazing and so very simple – *'love God and do whatever you please'* – how so? *'The soul trained in love to God will do nothing to offend the one who is to them, the Beloved'.*[3]

All our problems stem from lack of love, first for God, then others.

Owe no man anything but the debt to love.

"I am what I love, not what loves me" says Graham Cooke. He goes on to say *'This has become one of the most powerful identity statements that I have ever made. It has produced a*

freedom that has revolutionised my relationships.' (Living in your Truest Identity CD set)

Ready to proceed?

Notes
1. Thomas Paine, 'Common Sense' Pennsylvania February 14, 1776. Public domain.
2. 'The Greatest thing in the World', Henry Drummond, Revell a division of Baker Publishing Group, New Spire edition 2011 pp. 15-16.
3. Source www.wedgewords.wordpress.com

2

Presentation of the King

Whilst I was thinking and preparing this teaching I had a dream. In the dream I was trying on a shoe, it was soft as a glove, navy blue, sling back. It fitted my right foot perfectly, but I could not find the left one, even though in the dream I searched and searched.

This sent me to the Throne Room to find out why I only had one shoe.

The answer was simple. I only had half of what He wanted me to teach. I had the idea of the Sermon on the Mount, but I was missing the bit that went before.

Finding the other shoe, I began again.

The series is essentially about Majesty. HIS Majesty. The missing jewel in our theology.

It is all about – HIM and His Kingdom.

This is His season. *My dearest ones know that this season is My season.*

He is bringing us back to our centre, our focus, our Lodestar – that is something on which the attention is fixed.

Jesus Christ our risen, glorified and coming King.

This is not about us but about Him and His Kingdom that is progressively coming in our lives.

'God is most glorified when we are most satisfied in Him.' John Piper[1]

The following is an extract from the first chapter in my series entitled *'God, who is He?'* (you can find it on www.psalm131. com). It encapsulates what I sense God is saying at this time:

'The chief end of man is to glorify God and enjoy Him forever.'
(The Westminster Shorter Catechism)

Such a statement contrasts sharply with the humanistic philosophy of the world in which we live; what is being said is that creation exists for the glory of its Creator; that man is the crown jewel of creation, and as such, possesses a unique capacity to worship, glorify and honour his Maker.

The lost glory of this fallen world, and in some measure the church of Jesus Christ today, is that God is no longer central to our existence nor is He magnified and adored in the way He deserves to be.

A W Tozer in his little book 'The Knowledge of the Holy' says:

23

'The Church has surrendered her once lofty concept of God and has substituted for it one so low, so ignoble, as to be utterly unworthy of thinking, worshipping men. This she has done not deliberately, but little by little and without her knowledge; and her very unawareness only makes her situation more tragic...'[2]

It is imperative that we think rightly about God. This is not about us; this is about the Majesty of Heaven. Ours is to stand open mouthed in astonishment and wonder.

When Jesus walked the earth the first thing we find about Him when He was in the Temple as a young boy is, *they were astonished and amazed; they wondered* (Luke 2:47-50 KJV).

As He is released into His ministry on earth, they marvelled, they were astonished; they were in awe, they wondered. (Mark 1:27, Mark 2:12, Mark 5:20, Mark 5:42).

The healing of the human soul begins by restoring Him to His rightful place of amazement, astonishment, awe and wonder.

At Jesus' last interview on earth with the apostle John; we observe John's reaction when He sees the glorified, risen Lord, the One upon whose breast he had leant:

Then I turned to see the voice that was speaking with me. And having turned I saw seven golden lampstands; and in the middle of the lampstands I saw one like a son of man, clothed in a robe reaching to the feet, and girded across His chest with a golden sash. His head and His hair were white like white wool, like snow; and His eyes were like a flame of fire. His feet were like burnished bronze, when it has been made to glow in a furnace, and His voice was like the sound of many waters. In His right hand He held seven stars, and out of His mouth came a sharp two-edged sword; and His face was like the sun shining in its strength. When I saw Him, I fell at His feet like a dead man. (Revelation 1:12-17).

John sees with his physical eyes the glory of the risen Lord. And his reaction is not unusual – it is the norm for those who have seen Him, they fall down before the glory.

Abram sees and hears Jesus:

Abram fell on his face, and God talked with him. (Genesis 17:3 NASB).

He falls down before the glory.

His body also was like beryl, his face had the appearance of lightning, his eyes were like flaming torches, his arms and feet like the gleam of polished bronze, and the sound of his words like the sound of a tumult. Now I, Daniel, alone saw the vision, while the men who were with me did not see the vision; nevertheless, a great dread fell on them, and they ran away to hide themselves. So I was left alone and saw this great vision; yet no strength was left in me, for my natural colour turned to a deathly pallor, and I retained no strength. But I heard the sound of his words; and as soon as I heard the sound of his words, I fell into a deep sleep on my face, with my face to the ground. (Daniel 10:6-9 NAS).

Daniel falls down before the glory. He saw and heard 'awful' things. Awful: *a feeling of amazement and respect mixed with fear that is often coupled with a feeling of personal insignificance or powerlessness; the ability to inspire dread or reverence.*

That will be it.

We are all starved for His glory; the hunger in every human heart is for a return of the glory of God to its blazing, all consuming, fiery place at the very centre of our being.

We were created to worship Him in His glory...I fall down on my knees.

Notes
1. Desiring God, John Piper, 1995, Multnomah Books.
2. The Knowledge of the Holy, A W Tozer, 1978. Harper Collins, Preface p vii

3

Rescued

In 2010 thirty-three Chilean miners spent sixty-nine days nearly half a mile underground. These men lived the first seventeen days of their entombment ignorant of the fact that those looking for survivors did not know whether they were alive or dead under the 700 million tons of rock that had shifted.

Finally, and painstakingly the last man was lifted from the depths of the earth; they had all been rescued. There was great celebration. Each man had been delivered from certain death and given a new chance at life.

This absolutely describes our transfer from the kingdom of darkness, but many of us seem to have lost the dynamic of what took place; that we have moved from absolute darkness into the Kingdom of light ruled by the King of kings and Lord of lords.

The Bible uses the word *'rescue'* to describe how God delivered us from certain death into life:

He has rescued us from the domain of darkness and

transferred us into the kingdom of the Son whom He loves. (Colossians 1:13-14).

The word for 'transferred' originally meant deportation of a group of men or the removal of a group to form a colony. Paul says we have been transferred as a colony, a nation, from one kingdom into another.

Our King, Jesus, began His ministry with the emphasis on a Kingdom, the Kingdom of God:

Now after John had been taken into custody, Jesus came into Galilee, preaching the gospel of God, and saying, "The time is fulfilled, and the kingdom of God is at hand; repent and believe in the gospel." (Mark 1:14-15 NASB).

Jesus' teaching was filled with references to His Father's Kingdom, a Kingdom that according to His words, by His presence among us, had *'come near'*.

He said that His ability to cast out demons and heal the sick was proof that this Kingdom had come to those who listened to Him. (Matthew 12:28).

He made the Kingdom the theme of His preaching both before His death (Luke 4:43) and after His resurrection (Acts 1:3).

It was the focus of numerous parables: Mark 4:26 & 30; Luke 8:10; Luke 13:18-21 and is commended as a priority for our lives in Matthew 6:33 and Luke 12:31.

This is not only in the Gospels but also throughout the Acts of the Apostles and the Epistles. It is the *Kingdom* that has the priority.

It is displayed in righteousness, peace, joy and power, not in eating, drinking and talking. (Romans 14:17; 1 Corinthians 4:20).

The Kingdom is a very important subject to the King who is soon to come for His own. The Kingdom is a life to be lived and a future to be anticipated.

It is not dying and going to heaven. It is *'Thy will be done, on earth as it is in heaven'*.

How is it working out for you?

4

Making a mid-course correction

Something has to give here.

It is imperative that we make a mid-course correction, from our current self-centred Christianity to Christ-centred Christianity.

As we travel we will need to evaluate the reality of the Kingdom in our own lives. Are the ethics of the Kingdom our ethics for instance; are the values of the Kingdom our values?

Is the Kingdom what we seek first and foremost? If it is, you will be encouraged in your journey by these messages. If it is not, this will be a great place to start.

All these questions and more will be raised as we make our mid-course corrections, starting now.

The Kingdom is both a reality in the here and now and a promise to be inherited.

We, as a holy nation belonging to God are visible examples of the present and coming reign and rule of Jesus over His

Kingdom and His people (or we should be) as we sing –
'Christ in you, the hope of glory.'

Ours is a life to be lived and a future to be anticipated.

This is not about a passport to heaven, it is about a productive life now; a life that gives; a life lived to the full in the here and now and the prospect of future reward for a job well done. (Matthew 6:19-20).

It is not a 'me-centred' life; a self-referential life; but a life that pours itself out for others just our King showed us.

To understand all this, we will have to go back to basics and examine our fundamental beliefs to see if we are obeying the obvious requirements for entry into His Kingdom.

For instance, the need to be born again is foundational. Church attendance does not make you a Christian, nor does having parents who are Christian.

And neglected issues like His Lordship and water baptism, and I do not mean sprinkling, but full immersion.

Aah...

So before we start I will be addressing such questions as:

- Why is water baptism essential and what does it signify?
- What if He is Saviour, but not Lord? Does that make a difference?
- Are we born again simply to go to heaven or is there more

31

than this?

- Does God require a response from us beyond initial believing faith, if so, what is it?
- What does maturity look like?

And perhaps most importantly, are we in a prison from which we do not really wish to be set free?

For the answers to these and other questions, we are cleared for take-off, kindly fasten your seat belts…

5

Why be born again?

I will start by covering a basic issue: why we must be born again *from above.*

There does seem to be a misunderstanding here that we are really quite good people and all we need is enough attendances at church in order to collect enough tokens which will give us entry in to the Kingdom.

It is true that the remnant of the image of the Creator is still in fallen man, he is kind to an extent; he is good to an extent; he does love to an extent; but Romans tells us that not just some, but *all* have fallen short of the glory of God.

And Jesus told us:

> *"Truly, truly, I say to you, unless one is born of water and the Spirit he cannot enter into the kingdom of God. That which is born of the flesh is flesh, and that which is born of the Spirit is spirit. Do not be amazed that I said to you, 'You must be born again.'* (John 3:5-7 NASB).

Two things stand out here: the flesh and the Spirit, and water and the Spirit.

The prerequisite for entry into the Kingdom of God is that we must be born again of both water and the Spirit of God, and that henceforth we live from the Spirit not the flesh.

When Jesus spoke these words, He ushered in a new dispensation – the church age. Sent to His own who did not receive Him, He in turn sent His emissary, Paul, to preach the gospel to the Gentiles. These were good tidings of great joy.

Along the way somewhere we have lost the 'good tidings' and substituted them for 'ok' tidings. Our thrust now seems simply to get people inside the church building and keep them there by some means until their home call. Discipleship as Jesus taught has all but disappeared.

"You have heard it said… but I say to you." (Matthew 25:21-48)

When Jesus spoke these words, the Pharisees had no idea what He was talking about.

Indeed, there are many Christians today who would not understand the phrase *'the inner'* life. But this is just what Jesus came to give us.

He took us with Him on the cross at Calvary and nailed our old nature to the tree: it is our responsibility in the here and now to work out that death; from the outward show of religion, to the inward life of the Spirit.

This is the change that is coming beloved, from doing what we have always done, to realising the inner life, the spiritual life, where His indwelling presence becomes our reality.

Interested?

Read on…

6

Expiation

God had to do something radical to redeem us; to buy us back from the slave market of sin into which we were born. He took both the form of a man *and* the punishment we deserved for sin; it is called expiation.

A makeover would not do. He had to start over with us. Deal with the issue of sin that is inherent in us and give us a new start.

A new seed, a new DNA. Not paint and wallpaper.

To be born again we must first acknowledge that we are irretrievably lost and in a sinful state; buried in the dark. Like those Chilean miners we need someone to rescue us.

Having acknowledged our desperate need, we must do something about it by asking Him to rescue us from our degenerate, fallen state; to come into our hearts and lives and be our personal Saviour *and Lord.*

We know if we have made that request. We will probably remember the date quite clearly.

We do not drift into it nor are we christened into it. We make a conscious decision based on the facts. If that decision was made as a child we may wish to invite Him in as Lord now, as well as Saviour – grown up stuff.

God had to give us a completely new start, a new DNA, and that DNA was His own seed, placed in us at the moment of rebirth from above by His Spirit.

We now have dual nationality, we are both earthly and heavenly people. We are twice born, from above and below.

We influence the earth from our position in heaven.

When we became Christians we didn't *'make a commitment'* or *'a decision'.* We believed on the death and resurrection of the Lord Jesus Christ which set us free from the law of sin and death. We received forgiveness of our sins, which were many because we had a sinful nature. We got a new start. By the Holy Spirit we were given a new seed within us, the seed of incorruptible, eternal life. We now have a new nature and a new start.

We were translated from the kingdom of darkness into the Kingdom of light. The translation was legal and positional. That initial inrush of light is not all there is though.

We soon discover it is not so much getting us out of the world, as getting the world out of us. That is our biggest problem and this is exactly where the rubber hits the road. We discover some things about ourselves we would rather not know: we are rebellious, resentful, recalcitrant and independent by nature. We don't *want* God to rule over us.

Both seeds are still in us, one corruptible, the other, incorruptible; one from beneath the other from above.

This is where the battle for supremacy begins – His will or mine?

It is a bit like playing the board game, snakes and ladders; up a ladder and down a snake we go; throw a six to start again. It is our *choices* from this point on that will govern which seed we nourish and which seed will grow:

> *Your new life is not like your old life. Your old birth came from mortal sperm; your new birth comes from God's living Word. Just think: a life conceived by God himself!* (1 Peter 1:23 MSG).

That is a good place to stop, to give you the opportunity to think things through and assess your position on the board.

7

A glorious new life

I ended talking about snakes and ladders. A couple of little anecdotes may help your understanding here:

There is the story of the Indian gentleman who was converted and was asked by his pastor how his Christian walk was going. *'Well,'* he said *'it's like this, it depends which dog I feed, the black one or the white one'.*

You now have two natures, an old one and a new one. The old one is dead, it died with Christ on the tree, but the reality of that escapes most people, though it had not escaped this old Indian man.

Another illustration could be useful at this point:

I knew of someone who had a dream and this person did not like dogs; keep that in mind because it is important. In the dream they were scaling quite a steep hill and had nearly reached the top when they lost their footing and tumbled down to the bottom of the hill where they were met by a very friendly, large black dog, which made a great fuss of them, making it very clear he was pleased to see them back again and they were pleased to see the dog too.

It is the snakes and ladders I spoke about, this person was doing well, but suddenly, lost their footing; slid back into their old nature big time; went down the 'snake' and ended up being welcomed by the black dog of their old sinful nature.

The whole thrust in the New Testament about putting *off* this old nature and putting *on* the new one that is 'in Christ', is about the *shift* from:

- from the natural to the spiritual man;
- from the old DNA to the new;
- from the earthly to the heavenly;
- from Eros, self-referential love to Agape, self-sacrificing and self-giving love; the love of *choice* which seeks the best for others.

It is all about choices beloved, all about choices. This is why I likened it to a game of snakes and ladders – we dash up a ladder and within seconds plummet down a snake. Then wait there to throw a six to start again.

We call the old seed a multitude of things, the flesh, the carnal nature, the old Adam, the fallen nature, but essentially it is our *self-centred* nature that we inherited from the Fall.

And it is at war with God.
We discover we are in a prison cell but sometimes we do not want to leave because we are comfortable where we are.

Thy Kingdom Come

'The prison has been stormed, the gates of the prison have been opened, but unless we leave our cells and go forward in the light of freedom, we are still unredeemed...' Donald Bloesch.[1]

Someone I know had a dream. In it he was in a room fitted out with everything he liked, his favourite chair, his record collection, books and CDs, television, everything he could desire. The only down side was that the door had bars on it, but it did not seem to bother him too much, he was very comfortable. One day Jesus opened the door and came in, He invited the man to go with Him, they walked out into another room, it was vast, filled with glorious light and he knew, complete freedom; there was a huge Throne upon which the King would sit. The man looked around, thought for a moment and then turned and walked back into his cell closing the door behind him.

He was comfortable there. In his prison, familiarity and all that. He did not want to change.

We are sometimes more comfortable with bondage than with freedom. We are more comfortable with an outward show of religious fervour, than with inward transformation, because freedom comes at a price.

We have to leave the comfortable and familiar.

Keep that fact in mind as we travel along together. When we get to the law of re-relating you will understand more of what I mean.

In Romans 8:7, Paul says:

> *...the mind of the flesh [with its carnal thoughts and purposes] is hostile to God, for it does not submit itself to God's Law; indeed it cannot.*

Notice the words *'hostile'* and *'submit'*.

The carnal mind, the lower, un-renewed, unregenerate, mind, the fleshly mind and nature, will *not* bow the knee to God's reign and rule; it will *not* submit, it resists.

His Lordship versus our innate rebellion are the issues here.

We are fundamentally flawed. We are rebels. We need a new heart within us, a heart of flesh, not stone.

We are the prisoners of the giant of *self*. The tragedy is that even when we are born again we cannot see our true state, and sometimes when we do, we have no desire to escape from the cell in which we find ourselves. We are so comfortable with that black dog.

> *'Self is the only prison that can ever bind a soul'* Henry Van Dyke.[2]

I propose to show you the way out of this prison cell. I do not expect that all of you will choose to follow. I can tell you now that you will not like the route I will offer you but it is the only way to true freedom.

Those who choose it will be like the man in the film The

Matrix – taking the pill no one else would risk, and in so doing experiencing true freedom and reality.

To choose freedom will require leaving everything you understand right now behind and walking into a terrain that is completely foreign to you.

But you have your passport; it's up to date. You won't need a suitcase; you are wearing the clothing you need. You are clothed with the righteousness of Christ. You are about to find out exactly what that means.

A word of warning here, the culture is completely counter to the culture you are about to leave behind. That said, are you ready for a trip that is out of this world?

Let's go.

Notes
1. Quoted by Max Lucardo in 'He Chose the Nails' Thomas Nelson, p 50.
2. http://www.wiseoldsayings.com/prison-quotes/

8

There is another King

When we talk about a kingdom we presuppose there is a King.

When we pray what we call 'the Lord's prayer', we are speaking to a King and asking Him to do something:

"Thy Kingdom come, Thy will be done on earth, as it is in heaven."

Our Father, whom we are addressing here as both Creator and Redeemer, is right now restoring His Kingdom and His purpose on the earth.

This is His season.

A question: have you ever considered that what you are asking for when you pray is for the will of the King to be done in your life? That His *government* should come in your life, displacing your right to run the show?

Did you realise this and *is* that what you want?

Do you want to submit to a governmental authority other than your own?

Do you want to make Him *Lord* as well as Saviour?

Do you want to begin to train for eternity in the here and now?

> *But as many as received him, to them gave he power to become the sons of God, even to them that believe on his name.* (John 1:12 KJV).

He has given you the power; you have believed on His name, you are a babe, born again with the potential to become a fully mature adult.

There is an inheritance to be gained or lost. There are uncontrolled desires to be harnessed. There is both a crisis and a process involved here.

The crisis is that you are faced with something other than the status quo and you need to decide to take you further.

Your decision is between being a believer, follower or disciple; between radical renewal or business as usual.

The process is about getting to your destiny as a mature son of God; living from the DNA of your heavenly Father; coming into your inheritance.
It is being a disciple not just a believer or a follower. It is about coming into alignment with His will and letting go of yours.

45

When Jesus preached the Kingdom, He did not say *Believe on Me I am going to die for you and be your Saviour.* He said, *Repent, change your mind and direction of thinking, for the Kingdom of heaven is at hand.* (Matthew 4:17).

You are not saved just to go to heaven when you die – that is a given. You are intended to come to some kind of maturity in this life which fits you for your future in eternity, where you will reign and rule with Him as a fully mature son.

God's agenda for you is that you grow up – that is both your crisis and your process.

When He speaks in heaven the angels obey instantly, and we are asking that we might be the same. That this Kingdom, this place where He reigns and rules; where love is the key, may reside here in our hearts. That this culture may become our culture, because we are citizens of heaven and we have His DNA.

If we really want that life in the here and now we are in for some surprises along the way.

This Kingdom is universal and eternal; it is now and not yet. Currently it is inside us. (Luke 17:21).

It has a totally different culture and mindset.

Maturing means developing *Kingdom* responses to the situation's life will thrust you into. Your maturation process will affect everyone and everything around you.

To truly live our lives on earth as though we were there, will mean a complete transformation of our thinking. This Kingdom is upside down and it asks us:

- to die to live;
- to give rather than receive;
- to turn the other cheek;
- to go the extra mile,
- to forgive those who hurt us and despitefully use us;
- to keep no record of wrong;
- to bless when we are cursed;
- to give thanks at all times and in all circumstances for this is the will of God for us.

In my first book, School of the Spirit, we discovered that this King was altogether 'other than' us. He does not see things the way we do and He does not do things the way we do. He does not think the way we do.

> *"For my thoughts are not your thoughts, neither are your ways my ways," declares the Lord. "As the heavens are higher than the earth, so are my ways higher than your ways and my thoughts than your thoughts. As the rain and the snow come down from heaven, and do not return to it without watering the earth and making it bud and flourish, so that it yields seed for the sower and bread for the eater, so is my word that goes out from my mouth: It will not return to me empty, but will accomplish what I desire and achieve the purpose for which I sent it."* (Isaiah 55:8-11).

Next, we will begin to make some changes.

9

Preparation

If you are ready for this then, let us begin by praying what I call the 'Lordship' prayer that makes Him your Lord as well as your Saviour:

"Lord Jesus, I acknowledge my need of you and I accept you as my Saviour, my Deliverer and my Lord.

I invite you now to be the Lord (the authority, and to be in control of, and be the final decision maker) in the whole of my life.)

Lord of my human spirit and all my spiritual awareness and worship.

Lord of my mind, my attitudes, my thinking, my beliefs and my imagination.

Lord of my emotions and my expression of my feelings – anger, grief, joy etc.

Lord of my will and all my decisions.

Lord of my body, my physical health, my exercise, my diet, my rest and my appearance.

Lord of my sexuality and its expression.

Lord of my family and all my relationships.

Lord of my secular work and my Christian service.

Lord of my material goods and my perceived needs.

Lord of my finances.

Lord of my plans, my ambitions and my future.

Lord of the manner and timing of my death.

Thank you that Your blood was shed that I might be free from the consequences of sin and that my name is written in the book of life.

Amen."

If you prayed that with me, congratulations, you have just taken your first step towards freedom and becoming a disciple escaping from the trap of self-centeredness and stepping into the joy of self-forgetfulness.

10

The King and you

This series is about two people: The King and you...

When you were born again and were baptised, you came under a new government, under a new King whose Kingdom is eternal and unshakeable.

This Kingdom is now, and not yet. It is not visible. Most of its citizens have already gone on ahead of you.

Currently the Kingdom is within you. (Luke 17:21).

This King desires an intimate and very personal relationship with you. He calls you 'Bride'.

This is how He sees you:

> *"You are His treasure, a holy nation, His people, the people of His power, the people of His passion, the people of His heart, the people of His affection; you are more glorious than you know, stronger than you look, more brilliant than you can imagine – this is your identity; this is who you are – do not permit anybody*

talk you out of it or talk you down from that high place, that high calling. You are in Christ, you are astonishing; and at the very least you are wonderful, His marvellous darling..."
Graham Cooke,
'The Art of Thinking Brilliantly.' Audio series.

You belong to Him. You now have security, significance and self-worth. Be gone low self- esteem!

Everything the world seeks after has been freely given to you.

You no longer belong to this world; you are no longer captive to its culture. You have a new DNA. You are passing through on your way to the Eternal Kingdom. Your time here is training for that Kingdom.

Just as an infant's birth is but the beginning of its life, so your rebirth from above was the beginning of your journey into Christ and His Kingdom.

Your rebirth was but the start. Salvation was the first step. You were 'born again' *into* something. You were baptised *into* something.

God is purposeful and intentional towards you. He plans for eternity.

You now have an identity, a destiny, a purpose and an inheritance. You have a reason for living. You have a completely new DNA.

You have changed kingdoms. You have been transferred from the kingdom of darkness, into the Kingdom of His glorious light.

This Kingdom has but one law, the Royal law of love.

Your choices, or lack of them, will now govern your progress, or lack of it. Your attitudes will most definitely determine your altitude.

Your destination is heaven. Reigning and ruling with your King is your destiny and the Kingdom is within you.

The moment you were born again from above, *not of the will of man or the will of the flesh, but of God* (John 1:13), His Kingdom invaded your inmost being. Now it is a matter of regaining your own inner territory. This will require you to bring His Kingdom to bear upon every facet of your life and frequently act against yourself and your own desires.

It is about knowing Him. Not just on Sunday.

This King, you will quickly discover, does not do time-share. He comes to take over. He comes to reign and rule over your heart and life.

You have entered into a love affair. The love affair of the universe. The maiden in the Song of Songs declares: *'My beloved is mine'.* (Song of Songs 2:16)

It is not until the end of the book that she sees that *'I am my Beloved's'* (6:3). She has completely changed from possessing Him, as she thought she did at the beginning of her journey, to realising and revelling in His possession of her.

That is the journey upon which we are about to embark. From faltering love to mature love.

On our way we will find out:

- how He likes to do things;
- how we have to learn to 'process' what He is doing as we go from crisis to process;
- how He is not linear in His thinking but circular;
- how everything starts with Him and ends with Him and we are somewhere in the middle
- how what we behold, we will become.
- how He speaks not to the wimp in us but to the warrior.

Such an exciting journey to undertake. Take my arm then. Let's go *'follow the yellow brick road...'* [1]

Note
1. Y. Harburg, Wikipedia.

11

Unlearning

We do not have to travel far along this road before we discover that we do not know. We do not know anything. Zilch. Nada. Nothing.

First off, we do not know how to *behave* in this new kingdom.

We were familiar with the old nature, the old kingdom, and its culture, but this one has a completely different set of values, lifestyle and belief system; a totally different culture. Our old value system looked something like this:

We valued:

- Privacy
- Material success
- Convenience
- Comfort

Our new value system looks like:

- Openness and authenticity
- Sacrifice

- Love
- Discomfort

Our journey then is from the need for self-protection, privacy, material sufficiency and convenience to vulnerability, openness, sacrifice and personal loss that others may gain.

Living in the Kingdom we absorb the failures of others; love without reward; extend mercy; and suffer some.

The Kingdom is upside down. Our need to adjust is great. We quickly find that we thought we knew last week, we are certain we do not know this week.

It is not a new phenomenon when you *really* meet the King and His values. We find we tend to adopt the same position as Abram, Daniel and John – flat on our faces when we *really* see Him in His Majesty.

Nicodemus thought he knew, until he met with Jesus, and found out he really did not know anything at all. Least of all how he could enter this Kingdom. (John 3:1-17).

Unlike other kingdoms, this Kingdom is *unshakeable* and it never, ever changes. It is unshakeable because its King is immutable, and He never, ever, changes.

That means we are the ones who have to move our feet.

When the Holy Spirit treads on your toes *(insert your name here)* it is best to move your feet. This is probably going to be the greatest, longest and ongoing, lesson we will come up against as we learn not to argue, rationalise, justify, or excuse ourselves, but simply to change our minds about what we thought we knew. To move our feet.

> *'A long habit of not thinking a thing wrong, gives it a superficial appearance of being right, and raises at first a formidable outcry in defence of custom. But tumult soon subsides. Time makes more converts than reason.'*[1]

This is where we discover just how stubborn and rebellious we are by nature. How intractable. Peter had the same problem. Three times God had to drop the sheet before he got the message.

When we come to look at the difference between doing and being too, there may be major areas of change required.

Instead of being like Martha, cumbered about with much doing, we will be learning to be like Mary, sitting at His feet in an attitude of contemplation and rest; not doing anything unless He tells us, harder for some than others.

Could be quite a dramatic change here for some of us.

And the first thing we may find is that things do not happen when we speak, but when He does. We are so quick with the old verbals, even when we come into the Presence:

> *Do not be quick with your mouth, do not be hasty in your heart to utter anything before God. God is in heaven and you are on earth, so let your words be few.* (Ecclesiastes 5:2 NIV).

That, right there, is a very good piece of advice.

Time to learn to slow down, to focus on Him, to listen for His voice and wait for His touch. He initiates, remember, we respond.

So often, we get it the wrong way around and try to initiate things, or to 'wake Him up'. What a joke that is, we are the ones who need to awaken:

Awake, you who sleep, arise from the dead, and Christ will give you light. (Ephesians 5:14).

Interestingly the church at Ephesus was the one Jesus challenged about leaving their first love. They did not repent. There is no church there today.

"Remember therefore from where you have fallen; repent and do the first works, or else I will come to you quickly and remove your lamp-stand from its place – unless you repent." (Revelation 2:5).

The lamp stand (light) was removed.

He's *so* serious about first love. About us putting Him first so everything else falls in line behind.

Note
1. Thomas Paine, Common Sense, 1792

12

Behold, the Bridegroom comes

When the challenge went out it was the foolish virgins who were caught without any oil. They had lamps, a semblance of light, but no oil, no real illumination.

The word 'virgins' here is not about gender but about spiritual purity. These 'girls' were true to the God they believed in; they did not worship other gods, but they had no light and no oil.

Interesting that they *thought* they were prepared simply because they had a lamp, but the function of the lamp they had completely missed. Theirs would not give out any light when the time came.

The oil of course is the indwelling presence of the Holy Spirit. These 'girls' had the form, the letter, the lamp, but not the Spirit, the oil, the illumination, the revelation. They had bought into religion not relationship.

Learned men, Pharisees, Scribes and Sadducees, spent their whole lives studying the letter of the law, even prided themselves on it, but they knew nothing of the Spirit and it made them furious when they were found out.

Jesus comes to them and says *'You have heard it said, but I say to you'* cutting across everything they thought they knew.

They were furious! We do not like to be found out. What is more, they were not about to believe what He said, or change their ways.

This is the essence of the Sermon on the Mount. Jesus constantly says, *'You have heard it said... but I say to you...'* signalling radical change ahead.

Oh boy! Perhaps He is going to be saying similar things to us as we travel this road into a Kingdom lifestyle. Maybe there are going to be things about which we are so sure we would stake our lives, but when He comes with *His* light, we find we just do not know.

If you are teachable and mouldable at this point you will be rejoicing. If you are not you may be thinking you have read enough.

The choice is yours.

Didn't take us long before we were faced up again with that word did it? Choice.

It is what life in the Spirit is all about.

If you are still with the program, turn the page...

13

Mary and Martha

I do not remember anyone telling me when I was first born again that I now had a battle on my hands.

That there was another King and the king of self-will would need to be dethroned as two things cannot occupy the same space.

The Kingdom is about displacement. It comes in like a lion and displaces everything in its path.

It happened in Jerusalem when Jesus was born, Herod was troubled *and all Jerusalem with him.* (Matthew 2:3).

We get troubled when our apple cart is upset, if I can use that expression, and all our pet theories about Jesus and the Kingdom are turned on their heads.

As we saw in my first book *'The School of the Spirit'* we will find that He is altogether not like us. He says and asks things we do not like and that *will* upset our thinking.

He was made in the *'form of a man'* but there the resemblance really does end. He lived His life from the inside out. He lived His life to please only the Father.

He lived from His spirit, not His soul and His emotional and physical needs were the last things He was concerned about.

For us it is completely the opposite. We are all about getting our physical needs met, our prayers answered in the way we want. Pleasing the Father is not on our radar and our spiritual life goes hang most of the time.

In fact, many of us are totally unfamiliar with the concept of living from the inside out, from our spirit man; and being under new government.

Hopefully you will enjoy finding out the difference between your Mary and your Martha; between your soul and your spirit; between the old and the new; between self-will and His will.

Basically, it is the difference between living a life of constant conflict, anxiety and fear, and living a life of righteousness, peace and joy in the Holy Spirit; of living from the *opposite* spirit.

Remember in this Kingdom some of the things we do are to absorb human failure; love without reward; extend mercy; and suffer some. Cool.

Because He does not think like we do, or see things the way we do, He lives from the inside out and He wants us to live that way too. It takes time and a lot of adjustment in our attitudes and thought processes.

But it is part of what He won for us on the Cross. Part of our inheritance in Him.

He is circular in His thinking for a start. Everything begins with Him and ends with Him. Well it would wouldn't it? He created everything and there is nothing made that He did not make, so it stands to reason that it's a circle.

For of Him and through Him and to Him are all things, to whom be glory forever. Amen. (Romans 11:36).

The doxology, so called glory word, it is that all right!

14

Body, soul and spirit

So back to Mary and Martha.

I will call our spirit man Mary and our soul, Martha.

Mary is always at rest, sitting at the feet of Jesus, constantly worshipping. You may find yourself with a worship song in your mind when you wake in the morning that will be your spirit.

Martha, on the other hand, always has to *do* something, produce something; look back on the day to see what she has achieved. If she has not done anything, she is upset with herself.

Some of you already identify with Martha.

We should be a mixture of the two, but one will certainly be in the ascendency. All Mary and nothing gets done. All Martha and we leave our first love.

That was what Jesus had against Ephesus. He commended their works, but had against them that they had left their first love.

Mary is untroubled. She is in the rest of Hebrews 4: the rest we *'labour'* to enter. The *'labour'* is the fight we have against our old, carnal self; our unregenerate mind.

If you had not yet realised it, your soul does not give up its right to rule easily when it discovers there is another king!

To help understanding here, your soul is your mind, emotions and will. Your will is completely without feeling and goes wherever you direct, *'I will'* or *'I will not'*.

Your spirit on the other hand, is now under the benevolent dictatorship of the Holy Spirit. That is where we are aiming to live from, our spirit man, so we are always in alignment with Jesus.

There we live our lives in agreement with Him and are in constant connection and communion with Him as He desires.

The Holy Spirit indwells us both to will and to do. As a result, from time to time, we find a conflict of wills at work – His and ours.

Derek Prince says – *'the cross is where the will of God and my will cross…'* Quote from 'The Grace of Yielding', Derek Prince, p23 DP Ministries International 1977.

Selah – pause for thought.

15

This season is about Me

'Shoreless ocean, who can sound Thee
Thine own eternity is round Thee,
Majesty Divine'[1]

There is a sea change about to take place.

I told you at the beginning: *'My dearest ones, know that this season is MY season'* was a message I received from a very reliable prophetic source.

I knew immediately what God was saying:

- He is the Creator, we are the created;
- He is the King, we are His subjects;
- He is restoring things so they are the right way up.

For a long time we have been 'me' centred. Everything has been about 'me' knowing I am the beloved of God on whom His favour rests.

Now there has been a change of direction from the Throne Room, He is saying *'I want my enjoyment too'* and the emphasis must come back to His Lordship and His kingdom purposes for us.

His people will be the first to become aware of the change of season. He *always* tells His servants the prophets what He is about to do.

'The earth is the Lord's and the fullness thereof...'

Lordship, ownership, honour and glory and power belong to Him and Him alone. It is *all* His.

If we are to become Kingdom people, rather than church people, our whole philosophy of life will have to undergo a change of direction; we must get to know *Him*.

I want you to know Me; know My holiness; know My perfection; know My joy; know My love; know My goodness; know My plans;

I want you to know Me. I want you to know – *Me*. And I have given you My Holy Spirit for this express purpose.

'He must increase, but I must decrease.' (John 3:30).

'For me to live is Christ, and to die is gain.' (Philippians 1:21)

These words will become flesh upon us; not just words on a page and we need to remember just how He sees us because this is not going to be easy:

You are His treasure, a holy nation, His people, the people of His power, the people of His passion, the people of His heart, the people of His affection; you are more glorious than you know, stronger than you look, more brilliant than you can imagine – this is your identity; this is who you are – do not permit anybody talk you out of it or talk you down from that high place, that high calling. You are in Christ, you are astonishing; and at the very least you are wonderful, His marvellous darling...[2]

As we travel together we will not come out the same people we were when we went in.

We are about to learn about the culture of heaven so we may live properly here on earth before we arrive there. We will need to mind our manners – we are destined for the Throne.

Notes
1. *F W Faber, 'The Christian book of Mystical Verse' p.7; A W Tozer, Christian Publications Inc.*
2. 'Prophetic soaking' Graham Cooke.

16

What is heaven like?

Hear what a young friend of mine says:

First of all, it is important to understand what heaven is. When I was growing up, I saw it as a magical place in the sky, full of clouds where God lives. This perspective takes away the significance.

Heaven is God's Kingdom.

In being so, it is totally Holy, wonderfully magnificent. It is filled one hundred per cent with Majesty, and it radiates His glory.

It's not just where He resides, but where He alone reigns; sin, Satan and death don't have a speck of influence there.

This is why, to enter in the first place, we need the righteousness of Christ.

Heaven is totally about God. It is His matchless, everlasting Kingdom, and it is our home.

Thy Kingdom Come

Once we fully understand where we are from, we know who we are in Christ, and everything flows from that.

Our downside as humans is that we've grown up on earth.

We express the culture and customs of our worldly sovereign state.

It will take forever to wholly accustom to the culture of Heaven.

God wants to use us here on earth, we ain't got forever.

So here's the Good News.

You know who has spent forever in the Kingdom, and is accustomed to its culture? Jesus. So our new self, who is in Him, is the genius that already knows how to act like a citizen of Heaven.

Live in and through the new self and we will be ready.

This really encapsulates the journey; thanks Greg.

Thank You Father, for making it so clear. It is all about YOU. *'Thy Kingdom come'*

17

Acting against myself

This really is going to be a hard road. Until we regain dominion over our inner life and learn how to live from our spirit man, we are going to have to learn to act against ourselves, our fallen nature, all the time.

When the King faces us with choices, that is what happens. We have to choose *against* our former nature and choose *for* our new nature, every single time.

God wants to fill us with Himself and that means displacement. That which I thought and believed, must be displaced with Kingdom truth.

Acting against myself is a governmental transfer. The transfer of power from me, to Him. We talked about that didn't we?

I am saying and meaning, *'not my will, but Yours, be done Lord'.* We cannot say 'no' and 'Lord' in the same sentence.

In this Kingdom the way to life is death; the way to prosper is to give; the way up is down. It is upside down.

Consider this: *"Blessed are the meek, for they will inherit the earth."*

Meekness is not something we hear much about these days. Our culture seems to be *'he who shouts the loudest gets heard'*, but here Jesus is saying be meek.

Definition: to be humbly patient or docile under the provocation of others. (Dictionary.com)

Oh yeah! You don't know what my life is like. I do. Every circumstance is there to mature you in Christ.

Gentle, kind, ah – the fruit of the Spirit.

We see immediately there is a correlation between what Jesus is saying and the fruit of the Spirit. That which was imputed to us, His righteousness, is now being imparted to us; it is being worked in.

Notice it is His fruit, not ours. Our part is to move over and let Him live His life through us.

Bear *His* fruit, *through* us. Allow His government in us. It is all internal.

That is an example of acting against myself, letting His gentle nature rise to the surface from the Divine seed within us.

Father has given us a destiny and that is to be ambassadors or representatives of His nature in this life. However real heaven may be, the *governmental transfer* takes place here and now in this life, not when we get to heaven.

There will be no opportunities to be gracious there because there will be no difficult people or circumstances there. Bliss.

This is our training ground, our proving ground and our battleground.

Jesus sets us free from the need to act in our own interests rather than the interests of others.

In the Kingdom we are taught how to give to, serve, share and love others. To be there for them; putting ourselves and our needs to one side, knowing that all we need will be supplied if we seek first and only the Kingdom. (Matthew 6:33).

This is the way in which Father intends His will to come, to be accomplished, on the earth through us as we ask in the Lord's prayer.

Now we are beginning to see something.

18

Why water baptism?

Here we come with another challenge.

Water baptism.

Water baptism is a *governmental* transfer. It is very important. It is not an optional extra.

When Jesus came up out of the waters of baptism, the Jews around Him knew what was happening. They saw the statement He was making:

I am a representation of what God wants from this point on; you need to change masters.

He was just a normal human being at this time. He had not been crucified or glorified. Here is a man, a normal person, son of Mary and Joseph, making a proclamation to Israel that something new had come and that something was life changing.

It was a proclamation that a radical shift had occurred which would demand a personal and behavioural response from anyone who decided to follow Him.

Jesus had just proclaimed the manifesto of the Kingdom of God: *'Not My will but Thine be done'*.

Not my happiness and joy, but Yours, Father, is what I am here to fulfil. In response, His Father declared, *'This is My Son in whom I am well pleased.'*

By His immersion Jesus signified His willingness to do whatever His Father required to secure the return of the Kingdom; the reign and rule of God in the earth. He was about to take back the title deed which had been forfeited by Adam thus bringing the Father great joy.

The title deed to the planet was to be returned to its Creator. Adam had traded it for so-called knowledge in the Garden and plunged us under the government of Satan. Jesus wrested it back and to all who believe brought them in, under the Government of God.

Jesus came to do the will of the Father to redeem the world from utter darkness and return it to its rightful owner. Father's will included Jesus' death and resurrection.

What has this to do with water baptism you may ask. When we go through the waters of baptism we are declaring the same thing *'Not my will but Thine be done in my life. I symbolically die with You in baptism in order that I may live with You in resurrection life.'*

It is the first act which indicates we understand the implications of the Kingdom we have embraced; that we have made Him Lord of our lives, and now we are doing as He asks – be baptised.

It is our first declaration that we have been given freedom to *choose against ourselves* in the conflict between the kingdom of darkness and the Kingdom of Light into which we have now been transferred.

By baptism we are declaring we are no longer under our own government (which is that of Satan) but we accept the government of God in our lives, in just the same way as Jesus did. That from now on our greatest goal in life is pleasing the Father – and bringing Him joy.

We are showing we have moved from the kingdom of darkness into the Kingdom of Light.

We are acknowledging we have died to our old nature and lifestyle and we are rising in regeneration, newness of life, with the government of God upon us; that we are submitting to His Lordship.

We are agreeing with Him that *'it is no longer I that live, but Christ that lives in me'* (Galatians 2:20) and of His government there will be no end.

We embrace the fact that we are no longer our own; we have been bought with a price; we belong to Him.

From now on our lives will be characterised by choices – for or against Him and His light within us.

Water baptism is an act signifying a change of government.

Jesus says *'from 'now on your life will be My life, do what I am doing, live as I lived, to please My Father'.*

His love expects and requires us to learn to act and behave against ourselves, to mature to the point where we give ourselves away, just as He did.

It is both a process and a journey. Did you fully realise this at your baptism?

If you did not, you may wish to reflect on these things and consider being baptised again, this time in the full understanding of the statement you are making to God, to man and to the principalities and powers.

'I was like that, and now by God's grace, I am like this!'

Baptism is a cataclysmic act of spiritual warfare. It destroys the hold the kingdom of darkness had over you.

Arise and be baptised.

19

A Divine Confrontation

If you are still struggling with the issue of the importance of baptism, and I suspect some of you will be, this may help.

All that we have seen is summed up in one phrase: *'The government of God in our lives'*. Government implies both ownership and Lordship.

Many of us have never realised what took place when we were born again and many are not baptised.

Infant baptism, christening, dedication, is not enough. This is about someone who can decide for him or herself.

The baptism of which we speak is the baptism of a *believer* by plunging as if dyeing a garment; full immersion; under and up. Not sprinkling a baby who has no power as yet to make a choice for or against the truth.

The lack of understanding of the significance of baptism by full immersion has meant we do not co-operate with the Holy Spirit as He would like. We are still reserving the right to ourselves.

When we hear *'for me to live is Christ, to die is gain'* we think that was just for Paul or some super spiritual people.

But the fact is, the identification you go through when you are fully immersed is with the death of Christ and therefore His resurrection, that's why Paul told us to *reckon ourselves dead to sin but alive to God, in Christ.* (Romans 6:11).

When we come up from the water we have undergone a rite of passage that brings us under the Lordship of Christ, under His government, His headship. Just as Jesus, following His baptism, only ever did what the Father was doing and only ever saw things the way the Father did, so it will now be for us.

Your ultimate decision now is to agree with something that is already a fact.

When you are baptised, you signify you died and your life is now hid with Christ in God. (Colossians 3:1).

So how about it beloved? Is it time for full immersion if you haven't already done so?

He never coerces or forces us. I will leave you to think about that one.

20

Conversion

'Many souls are saved but never converted.'

The Lord told me this a long time ago and I have pondered it over the years.

To be converted means you make an about turn, a complete change in direction.

Many are believers, or followers but not disciples. Disciples have turned. And go on turning.

This is an excerpt from a series of mine on the website www. psalm131.com, entitled 'As grows a tree', chapter 8 'Turnings':

'Many of us received the Good News without appreciation and salvation without repentance; we have obtained facts without enthusiasm and received Christ without passion; we are saved, but our hearts have never fully turned towards Him in absolute surrender and devotion. As a result, we live at a distance from Him without intimacy or a close encounter; paradise which was lost is not yet fully regained... we still keep tight control of our lives.

We declare we know Him and proclaim He is our Lord but a closer examination of how we live that out reveals something different; in actuality we keep vast areas from Him – either from fear or unbelief – we are divorced from the truth that in Him, and *only* in Him, we live and move and have our being.

Like the Israelites before us, we forget when we come into the land of plenty

*Then it shall come about when the Lord your God brings you into the land which He swore to your fathers, Abraham, Isaac and Jacob, to give you, great and splendid cities which you did not build, and houses full of all good things which you did not fill, and hewn cisterns which you did not dig, vineyards and olive trees which you did not plant, and you eat and are satisfied, then watch yourself, that you do not forget the Lord who brought you from the land of Egypt, out of the house of slavery. You shall fear only the Lord your God; and you shall worship Him and swear by His name. You shall not follow other gods, any of the gods of the peoples who surround you, for the Lord your God in the midst of you is a jealous God; (*Deuteronomy 6:10-15 NASB)

The Spirit of God yearns jealously over us for the entire devotion of our heart.

Our desire to maintain independence from God and be masters of our own destiny is a legacy from the Fall, for without Him we can do nothing.

Disciples know and understand the full importance of the Gospel, the good news, not the mediocre news. They have laid down their independence and appropriated all that Christ won for them on the Cross.

They recognise and embrace the fact that there are no longer two lives to be lived but one. They have had a completely new start. Not a makeover. A new start. His life for mine.

Everything under His government and control, even though it is difficult at times, you have your constant companion, the Holy Spirit, to teach and guide you.

He is just like Jesus. He is the Spirit of Jesus; He is co-equal and co-eternal with the other members of the Godhead, They are indivisible –

Romans 8:9 '*But you are not in the flesh but in the Spirit, if indeed the **Spirit of God** dwells in you. Now if anyone does not have the **Spirit of Christ**, he is not His.*'

Wonderful. It is like walking with Jesus every day.

"I will send you another Comforter" Someone who is just like Me.

And He did. We have all we need to live this thing.

It is true, it takes a lifetime to produce the Christ life in us, but the journey of a thousand miles starts with the first step.

We *do* have a fallen nature that wants to fight back every

step of the way. We *are* rebels at heart. But He has given us a new one of those. We can say 'yes' to Him and mean it as we learn to live from our new man.

He has something very precious He wants us to have. *Dominion*.

God wants us to take back that dominion we lost at the Fall, and He starts with our own inner territory. Getting control, dominion over ourselves.

Unless we recognise this enmity, this warfare, that rages within and how important it is that we align ourselves with Him in everything, we are doomed to stay in a place where the enemy can use us to play football with any time he wishes.

Lunch is served and you are on the menu.

Every time you protect yourself, for instance, you go into the enemy's territory. Self-protection.

'I did it my way' was Adam's theme tune.

You can throw a tantrum a week and walk away from God any time if you want to; He won't love you any the less. Just be aware that the lovely red carpet and white sofas means you have walked into the lion's mouth. That's his tongue and his teeth you're looking at and the trap is about to close on you – again.

The choice is yours.

You can be *'tossed about with many a conflict many a doubt, fightings within and fears without...'*[1] Or you can grow up and live in resurrection life, running towards Him every time you have a problem.

Everything we have looked at so far presupposes that you understand this and have made the choice.

That is why I brought you to that place of seeing the significance of water baptism. So that you might see your own resistance to the government of God, and make a choice.

God sees you as already dead and risen in Christ.

The question is how do you see yourself?

Getting this sorted could revolutionise your Christian walk and bring great joy as we move on to look at how living a Kingdom lifestyle will affect every aspect of your life, if you allow it.

Note
1. *'Just as I am'* Charlotte Elliott, Redemption Hymnal number 354.

21

Relationships

As we go along you will find this series is all about relationships, primarily between God and you, then you and yourself, and finally you and other people.

Most of our problems we find are with other people. If they would just do what we want, when we want, be different, not so irritating, there would be no problem, sigh, but there you are, they just need correcting.

Was that last statement true or false??

Of course, we all know that it *isn't* other people, it is us that is the problem. Mostly if we are not out with God, we are out with ourselves, which leads to us being out with those around us.

There is a huge internal conflict going on.

Peace you know is the cessation of conflict in the human will; you are no longer fighting the God who is within you. So, your peace level is an indicator to how much you are wrestling with the Holy Spirit right now.

Thy Kingdom Come

Come on, let's have some honesty here!

On a scale of 1 to 5, with five being so peaceful you will fall off your perch, just how peaceful are you right this moment? Be honest, no one else can see – except Him of course!

Any dis-peace is your fallen nature fighting for supremacy.

We have some growing up to do, and it would be good if we got a move on. The first person we get right with is God Himself and He does it.

He sends His Holy Spirit into our lives and we are born again from above. We have the equipment to overcome ourselves.

But that is only the beginning of the story. At least it should be, unfortunately many of us have gained the impression that it is the whole story and we have not moved on since the day of our conversion.

Therein lies the key to the problem James highlighted:

Where do you think all these appalling wars and quarrels come from? Do you think they just happen? Think again. They come about because you want your own way, and fight for it deep inside yourselves. You lust for what you don't have and are willing to kill to get it. You want what isn't yours and will risk violence to get your hands on it.

You wouldn't think of just asking God for it, would you? And why not? Because you know you'd be asking for

*what you have no right to. You're spoiled children, each
wanting your own way.* (James 4:1-3 MSG)

Left to ourselves we are weak, twisted and deceitful people.
We are beyond repair.

Discernment has become judgement; love has become
'what's in it for me'. We desire to acquire, possess and control
situations and people around us.

If you do not believe me, just spend some time asking Father
for yourself. You need to be convinced about the changes we
need to make before we go any further.

We are about to strip away all the nice form and religiosity we
take comfort in and hide behind and what will be revealed is
not a pretty sight!

When the scripture starts to open our inner man and show
us exactly what we are it is painful, but it applies to us all.
Take comfort in the fact that it has hit me before it hits you
and the truth when it first comes normally receives a negative
response.

We are in for some road-blocks ahead I suspect, but if you
can do violence to yourself you will find another 'true' self,
emerging that you will love and so will those around you, and
Jesus, well He will see the travail of His soul and be satisfied.

Gird up the loins of your mind then, as one of the apostles
has said, and let's do this thing.

Thy Kingdom Come

God has given us all we need for a life of godliness; let's walk right into it.

22

His Divine Power

Shoreless ocean, who can sound Thee?
Thine own eternity is round Thee,
Majesty Divine.[1]

From time to time we need to bring ourselves back to our centre. Christ and Him crucified.

To focus quite deliberately on the One who saved us and called us into His eternal Kingdom. To remember that eternal life is about knowing *Him* and Jesus Christ whom He sent.

Focus. On Him and *His* divine power. You cannot do this without Him. He has made sure you cannot.

The demands of the Sermon on the Mount require supernatural intervention, that is why some theologians have said it is not for this life, but the next! They left out the necessity of experiencing the indwelling of the Holy Spirit not just in the rebirth, but also in the power from on high.

If you are not baptised in the Holy Spirit, stop right here and humbly ask Him to come into you in power as He did at Pentecost, so that His purposes might be fulfilled on the earth in you and through you.

He will be *so* happy to come to you. You cannot do this without Him. It is His power that will get the job done, not your will power, or won't power; not all your determinations to do better next time, but His power indwelling you as you yield to His dominion.

We do well to remember at this point that He extracts from us in a time of war (inner conflict) what we gave Him in a time of peace.

We will encounter that a great deal in our fight for dominion over self and its incessant demands.

Ah... that word again, dominion. That which He gave Adam and that which Adam lost.

Peace with God and dominion over self; that which Jesus, the Second Adam, has regained, the restoration of peace with God and dominion over ourselves.

Now we are embarking on our journey to regain our own inner territory by keeping in step with the Holy Spirit and pushing back the giants, which we will encounter in our own lives.

Giants like: look good, feel good and be right; be first, best and right – that competitive spirit of which we are so proud.

Giants like the desires for position, possession and power. Giants like remaining undisturbed.

We are waking the dead here. Good book that 'Waking the Dead' by John Eldridge. I recommend it.

He has given us all we need to press into our Promised Land, our Land of Promises. Hear what Peter has to say about it all:

Simon Peter, a bondservant and apostle of Jesus Christ,

To those who have obtained like precious faith with us by the righteousness of our God and Saviour Jesus Christ:

Grace and peace be multiplied to you in the knowledge of God and of Jesus our Lord, as His divine power has given to us all things that pertain to life and godliness, through the knowledge of Him who called us by glory and virtue, by which have been given to us exceedingly great and precious promises, that through these you may be partakers of the divine nature, having escaped the corruption that is in the world through lust.

Fruitful Growth in the Faith

But also for this very reason, giving all diligence, add to your faith virtue, to virtue knowledge, to knowledge self-control, to self-control perseverance, to perseverance godliness, to godliness brotherly kindness, and to brotherly kindness love. For if these things are yours and abound, you will be neither barren nor unfruitful in the knowledge of our Lord Jesus Christ. For he who lacks these things is shortsighted, even to blindness, and has forgotten that he was cleansed from his old sins.

Therefore, brethren, be even more diligent to make your call and election sure, for if you do these things you will never stumble; for so an entrance will be supplied to you abundantly into the everlasting kingdom of our Lord and Saviour Jesus Christ. (2 Peter 1:1-11)

From time to time we must bring ourselves back to *His* Divine Power.

To reassure ourselves that His is the power and the glory forever and ever Amen. He has already given us all the things that pertain to both life and godliness. Our job is to press in and keep pressing in until the territory is gained.

Next time we will start to have a look at the things that hold us back. Meanwhile I will leave you with this thought:

Discipline in a Long-Distance Race

Do you see what this means – all these pioneers who blazed the way, all these veterans cheering us on? It means we'd better get on with it. Strip down, start running – and never quit! No extra spiritual fat, no parasitic sins. Keep your eyes on Jesus, who both began and finished this race we're in. Study how he did it. Because he never lost sight of where he was headed – that exhilarating finish in and with God – he could put up with anything along the way: Cross, shame, whatever. And now he's there, in the place of honour, right alongside God. When you find yourselves flagging in your faith, go over that story again, item by item, that long litany of hostility he ploughed through. That will shoot adrenaline into your souls!

In this all-out match against sin, others have suffered far worse than you, to say nothing of what Jesus went through – all that bloodshed! So don't feel sorry for yourselves. Or have you forgotten how good parents treat children, and that God regards you as his children?

My dear child, don't shrug off God's discipline,
but don't be crushed by it either.
It's the child he loves that he disciplines;
the child he embraces, he also corrects.

God is educating you; that's why you must never drop out. He's treating you as dear children. This trouble you're in isn't punishment; it's training, the normal experience of children. Only irresponsible parents leave children to fend for themselves. Would you prefer an irresponsible God? We respect our own parents for training and not spoiling us, so why not embrace God's training so we can truly live? While we were children, our parents did what seemed best to them. But God is doing what is best for us, training us to live God's holy best. At the time, discipline isn't much fun. It always feels like it's going against the grain. Later, of course, it pays off handsomely, for it's the well-trained who find themselves mature in their relationship with God.

So don't sit around on your hands! No more dragging your feet! Clear the path for long-distance runners so no one will trip and fall, so no one will step in a hole and sprain an ankle. Help each other out. And run for it!

Work at getting along with each other and with God. Otherwise you'll never get so much as a glimpse of God. Make sure no one gets left out of God's generosity. Keep a sharp eye out for weeds of bitter discontent. A thistle or two gone to seed can ruin a whole garden in no time. Watch out for the Esau syndrome: trading away God's lifelong gift in order to satisfy a short-term appetite. You well know how Esau later regretted that impulsive act and wanted God's blessing-but by then it was too late, tears or no tears. (Hebrews 12:1-17 MSG)

Amen.

Note
1. *'Majesty Divine' F W Faber, p 7 'The Christian book of Mystical Verse' Martino Publishing 2010*

23

Jesus is counter-culture

We have to launch in somewhere and the Ten Commandments that were reinterpreted by Jesus in His teaching on the Mount, is a good place to begin.

He did not do away with them – the Commandments – He brought them closer. He dealt with them in the heart of fallen man and showed us a more excellent way.

In this liberal society where anything goes, where there is no absolute truth and God is more enlightened than He was when He wrote the Bible, don't think that God has lowered His standards somehow.

What you will find is that He has not changed at all; because He is immutable.

I the Lord change not. (Malachi 3:6)

What has happened is that we are accustomed to our culture. And this is where the real shock of what it means to belong to the King and be a citizen of His Kingdom, really hits us right where we live.

Jesus is *totally* counter-culture. For instance, turn the other cheek; give to those who ask you, don't repay evil for evil; do good to those who hurt you; forgive all the time; the list goes on and on.

Getting the drift?

If you truly follow Him you will be counter-cultured too. You will not fit. But you will rejoice in the fact that you don't.

Then you will not do an Esau and trade your inheritance for a bowl of soup.

Once you begin to see what it means to live as a citizen of the Kingdom of God; that you are no longer earth bound; that you aren't a turkey, you are an eagle; nothing will stop you from soaring higher and higher.

Cleared for take-off!

24

Love and self-control

If you look even cursorily at the fruit of the Spirit you will note that seven are held in by two – one at each end like bookends; love and self-control.

Without these two the others will not develop.

Love and self-control.

The Ten Commandments are split: four towards God & six towards our fellow men. Our loveless attitudes towards others and our uncontrolled nature are thrown into relief as we examine them.

Human nature being what it is, I only have to say to you *'don't touch that'*, or *'please do it this way'* for you to disobey so soon as my back is turned. Right?

Anyone brought up a child? *'Leave that alone while I'm out!'* Do they? I think not.

God gives just one test command to Adam – *'don't eat that fruit'* – what happens? You fill in the blank.

Multiply that. He now gives ten of the same; no chance! We are undone.

This is where we really see what rebels we are.

'If you love Me, you will show it by doing ten things.'

I will give you one. Try the first for a start.

You shall love the Lord your God with all your heart, soul, mind and strength. (Deuteronomy 6:5).

Are you doing that yet? Answers on a postcard please.

The law, Paul says, just shows us we cannot keep it. It is the schoolmaster to lead us to Christ.

'There was a young lady from Niger,
Who smiled as she rode on a tiger.
They returned from the ride,
The young lady inside and
The smile on the face of the tiger.' Anon.

He who rides a tiger, it is said, can never get off. We ride a tiger. It is called our old nature; the old Adam.

The Sermon on the Mount will reveal everything in us that needs to be changed.

Every stiff-necked response; every refusal to change; every stamp of the foot; every petulant cry; every tantrum, will show where the wellspring of our life really, really is – little 'ol me.

He knows what He is getting, and He does not love us any the less. But He requires us to change.

There is something we need to do, something that is our responsibility, yield to His dominion and in so doing; we regain our dominion over self and our sinful nature.

Seems like a good deal to me. What do you think?

25

Embracing change

We saw that going through the waters of baptism was an act of violence against ourselves. We were making a public declaration that we were going from darkness into light, from living our lives for ourselves to living them for the One who redeemed us by His blood.

We are His purchased possession.

You have to beat the devil on the level you are on. But first, you must conquer the enemy within. The beastie of the self-referential nature.

Why? We no longer belong to ourselves. The transaction has been done.

Darkness is not just obvious things like cults; the moral confusion that abounds in the world, but it is our love for ourselves that spins us off into darkness.

Self-government, independence, self-protection is what is being nailed here.

My opinion, *my* best interests, what I want, *my* plan for *my* life. These are implicitly yielded to the authority of another as we go under the water.

The act of baptism takes us out from under the authority of darkness into the kingdom or the governmental sphere of authority of the Kingdom of Light.

Because it is governmental, it eventually becomes behavioural.

It is here we start to rewrite or reinvent ourselves and this process will go on incrementally; what we see from the basement of life is different from what we will see from the penthouse.

We will come to this place at regular intervals now, so it is good that we recognise this soon and become faster in our ability to move our feet and go the way of the Spirit.

For example:

Peter, here he is on the roof top thinking about lunch; he went up to pray but he is thinking about food. Suddenly his reverie is interrupted and this sheet comes down full of animals. Peter, good Jewish boy, would not touch any of them. (Acts 10:11-16). *Forbid it Lord!* is his initial reaction.

Three times God has to show him the sheet before he gets the message. *I'm sending you to those you consider unclean Peter – the Gentiles.*

Ah! Light.

What am I saying? When you get to a new place the *light* is a shock. When you hear something new you most often think it must be wrong and you take some persuading!

The truth, remember, when it first comes is almost always received negatively. It is the human condition.

But when we get to a new place we have a lot to unlearn and the sooner we recognise that we really *do not* know, the better. The way we have always done things gets in the way of the better way.

Peter had been lifted onto a higher plane. At first he resisted, but when he became accustomed to what God was saying and some understanding came, he embraced the change.

When God moves us, we start to see things differently, our language changes. He becomes something new for us He has not been before. Yes the enemy is bigger, but he is there so you grow to be as big as him, put your foot on his neck, and use him to elevate you to the next level.

And so, it goes on.

> *'You cannot take ground from the enemy if he has ground in you. Cleaning and clearing our own house is a vital part of our own self-control and personal discipline.'*[1]

And that old nature, when you keep nurturing it, is the enemy's playground. It depends which dog you feed remember? Now we cannot have that can we?

Next time we will begin to take some baby steps in the right direction.

Note
1. 'Qualities of a Spiritual Warrior' Graham Cooke p 36 Brilliant Book House, 2008.

26

Unlearning – Saul

I talked last time about Peter and his experience with the sheet; his culture shock that God had included the Gentiles in the gift of salvation, and that He was sending him to them.

But there comes someone else on the scene that had perhaps an even bigger shock. Saul of Tarsus, who became Paul the apostle to the Gentiles:

> *Imagine this: Suddenly a light flashes from the sky around Saul, and he falls to the ground at the sound of a voice.*
> *The Lord: Saul, Saul, why are you attacking Me?*
> *Saul: Lord, who are You?*
> *Then he hears these words:*
> *The Lord: I am Jesus. I am the One you are attacking. Get up. Enter the city. You will learn there what you are to do.* (Acts 9:3-6 The Voice).

These are shocking, unexpected words that will change his life forever.

This man perfectly illustrates the difference between an intellectual knowledge of Jesus and an experience. Between an intellectual theologian and a relational theologian if you like.

Shocking, unexpected, the words change his life forever.

There is an old saying that *'a man with an experience is beyond reason'.*

Saul of Tarsus, arrives on the scene in Acts, breathing out threats, killing Christians, and completely convinced that he was doing God's will. He was a Hebrew and proud of it. Knew all there was to know about the law.

Now he has to undergo a most painful lesson, which breaks not only his pride in his so-called knowledge, but his self-sufficiency.

Paul was an intellectual theologian. He *'knew by the hearing of the ear, but* **now** *his eyes see Him'* as Job said. (Job 42:5 emphasis added).

The first thing that happens is Light. Then he is knocked down. And out; he's lost his sight. Finally, he sees, and what he sees causes him to repent big time.

He just had an experience and He now knows that what he thought he knew, he surely didn't know.

Just like Peter.

Thy Kingdom Come

As we travel together, we may find that the shock to our system is every bit as severe as it was to these two men, who left the very word of God to us as a legacy.

It is about unlearning what we thought we knew.

Better fasten your seat belts again.

27

Encountering Majesty

Change is what happens when we encounter Majesty. When we experience Him.

Paul knew, Peter knew and Mr. Beaver says so, and he should know:

> *"Aslan is a lion – the Lion, the great Lion." "Ooh" said Susan. "I'd thought he was a man. Is he – quite safe? I shall feel rather nervous about meeting a lion"*
> *"Safe?" said Mr. Beaver "Who said anything about safe? 'Course he isn't safe. But he's good. He's the King, I tell you."*[1]

'He's the King, I tell you.'

If it is safety you are after, exit now. His Majesty is good, very good, but there is no way He is safe. You always know where you are with Him.

You never know what He is going to do next. For those of us who are control freaks, that poses a real problem. That is why we are so reluctant to make Him Lord of our lives. It feels like letting go of control, which of course it is.

No longer two lives to be lived, but one, and the One knows where He is headed. Problem here is, we have not got a clue and He has got the map!

Again, C. S. Lewis comes to our rescue. Jill is lost in a scary forest, she cries and cries and develops a terrible thirst. As she looks for water, she happens upon a stream and eagerly runs toward it, but then – she notices a Lion is lying beside it:

'She stops in her tracks. The Lion, knowing she is thirsty, invites her to come and drink...

"'May I – could I – would you mind going away while I do?' said Jill.

The Lion answered this only by a look and a very low growl. And as Jill gazed at its motionless bulk, she realised that she might as well have asked the whole mountain to move aside for her convenience. The delicious rippling noise of the stream was driving her nearly frantic.

'Will you promise not to – do anything to me, if I do come?' said Jill.

'I make no promise' said the Lion.

Jill was so thirsty now that, without noticing it she had come a step nearer.

'Do you eat girls?' she said.

'I have swallowed up girls and boys, women and men, kings and emperors; cities and realms' said the Lion. It didn't say this as if it were boasting, nor as if it were sorry, nor as if it were angry. It just said it.

'I daren't come and drink,' said Jill.

'Then you will die of thirst,' said the Lion.

'Oh dear!' said Jill, coming another step nearer, 'I suppose I must go and look for another stream then.'

'There is no other stream.'

Said the Lion.' [2]

C S Lewis puts these words into the mouth of Aslan, the Christ figure, as he talks to a frightened little girl. There is no other stream…

'Lord where else can we go, you have the words of eternal life'. (John 6:68)

Ever noticed that He extracts from us in a time of war what we gave Him in a time of peace?

'I make no promise' the Lion said – concerning what? The Lion makes no promise that Jill will not suffer if she comes to drink.

All our efforts at control are prompted by self-preservation. The cross does not take prisoners, it kills you.

What I am doing here is softening you up for what is to come. Leaving all to follow Christ

Now great multitudes went with Him. And He turned and said to them, "If anyone comes to Me and does not hate his father and mother, wife and children, brothers and sisters, yes, and his own life also, he cannot be My disciple. And whoever does not bear his cross and come after Me cannot be My disciple." (Luke 14:25-27).

Death on the instalment plan!

Notes
1. C. S. Lewis, 'The Chronicles of Narnia' – p 75 'The Lion, The Witch and The Wardrobe', Diamond Books 1998.
2. C. S. Lewis, 'The Chronicles of Narnia' pp 23, 24 'The Silver Chair' Diamond Books 1998.

28

Death on the instalment plan

Here we come again with discipleship and Jesus lays out the cost – forsaking all and bearing a cross. Not putting it round your neck, but dying on it:

Dying with Jesus, by death reckoned mine; Living with Jesus a new life divine: [1]

This is not literal physical death. It is very unlikely that you will be called to martyrdom, but the death Paul speaks about in Romans 6:11.

Death on the instalment plan; dying daily. The death we underwent in baptism; we now reckon ourselves alive to God in Christ, and give no more heed to the old nature and the old way of life.

Disciples are the ones who accept this and continue with Him in His trials.

You cannot avoid them, trials that is. They are there to strengthen you in your faith and show you something more of what He wants to be for you in that particular situation.

If you process them properly, you come out the other side with a different version of yourself.

Crisis to process, that is the way we go. We need to ask some intelligent questions not just scream to be released from the situation.

Questions like:

- Is this You?
- Is this the Cross?
- Am I reaping what I have sown?
- Is this the devil?
- Are you nailing something in my life?
- Am I missing something here?
- And of course, the basics:
- 'What does this mean?
- What should I do?'

All bring you into an intimate conversation with Him, which is what He is after. Intimacy.

Maybe the purpose of your current trial is simply to get your attention so that He can love you and give you something more of Himself; it is His way of getting your attention – just a thought.

Which I will leave you with today.

Note
1. 384 Redemption Hymnal, D. W. Whittle.

29

The One-eyed man

'In the kingdom of the blind the one-eyed man is king'.

The Holy Spirit kept repeating this phrase finally I got what He was pointing at:

"Do not lay up for yourselves treasures on earth, where moth and rust destroy and where thieves break in and steal; but lay up for yourselves treasures in heaven, where neither moth nor rust destroys and where thieves do not break in and steal. For where your treasure is, there your heart will be also.

The Lamp of the Body

"The lamp of the body is the eye. If therefore your eye is good, your whole body will be full of light. But if your eye is bad, your whole body will be full of darkness. If therefore the light that is in you is darkness, how great is that darkness!

You Cannot Serve God and Riches

"No one can serve two masters; for either he will hate the one and love the other, or else he will be loyal to the one and despise the other. You cannot serve God and mammon.

Do Not Worry

"Therefore I say to you, do not worry about your life, what you will eat or what you will drink; nor about your body, what you will put on. Is not life more than food and the body more than clothing?" (Matthew 6:19-25).

The whole passage is about finance, money, wonga, dosh and what we do with it.

And it is about the heart and the eye.

Storage in those days it would seem was fraught with the same problems as it is in the 21st century – moth, rust and thieves!

It is about light and darkness; the futility of storing anything on earth versus the value of storing treasure in heaven.

The heart and the eye here are closely tied to the spiritual as well as the physical realm. The good eye is one that is generous towards God and man. The bad eye essentially is the one that has turned away from God and is watching out for itself.

We have to ask ourselves some questions.

- Where's my focus?
- Where do I put my treasure?
- Is it all about my needs?
- Or am I looking beyond that?

If you focus, He says, on storing up for yourselves things (stuff), in this life, your treasure will be there. If your eye is single, in other words, if you are focussed on My kingdom, you will be full of light, but if you are focussed on earthly things, the reverse is true.

He ends by saying you cannot serve two masters, it has to be one or the other; the kingdom of darkness or the kingdom of light. Your life is more than just what you stand up in. You are an eternal being and you should be laying up treasure for eternity, not for the here and now.

Paul, in his letter to the Colossians, says the same thing:

If then you were raised with Christ, seek those things which are above, where Christ is, sitting at the right hand of God. Set your mind on things above, not on things on the earth. For you died, and your life is hidden with Christ in God. When Christ who is our life appears, then you also will appear with Him in glory. (Colossians 3:1-4 NKJV).

The issue here is not so much about money per se, but about how you view it. If obtaining it and what it can get you is your goal, you are out of focus. You need a lens change.

Money and how you view it, is key in the life of a disciple. You *cannot* serve two masters.

Being consumed with making money could be construed as *'the cares of this world and the deceitfulness of riches…'* which we know, choked the good seed in one of Jesus' parables.

You cannot seek material sufficiency and the Kingdom at the same time – remember the world's values and the kingdom values?

Allow me to remind you of number two on the world's list: Material success.

One of our most important lessons could be that our finances are spiritual!

30

Giving is spiritual

You and I are building for eternity and we must watch the building materials we use. Are they wood, hay and stubble, or gold, silver and precious stones? (1 Corinthians 3:12-13).

Preoccupation with anything less than God in this life causes darkness and confusion right across our lives, not just in the area of giving.

Our focus must be on Him in all things and at all times, or we will miss the higher path.

In Jesus' teaching on the parable of the good seed and the harvest, it was not necessarily sin that caused the seed to be choked. It could have been the thorns and briars of constant demands on finances from 'worthy' causes that were the source of unfruitfulness, not necessarily profligate living.

We have already given the Lord our finances when we prayed the 'Lordship' prayer, but each individual situation must now be brought under His scrutiny.

There is no shortage of 'worthy' causes but it is the ones He wants to assist that we need to find and give to.

We must also bring our own private spending under His control. I find that what I thought I needed (read – must have) is not really important at all.

God has a plan for your finances and it may well not line up with your plan, but hey, you are under new management.

Personally, I have swallowed hard on a number of occasions when Father has asked me to give more than I really wanted to in a direction I did not think right anyway!

I have never refused Him. Do I lack anything? No. He is the source of my provision and therefore the source of my direction in how I distribute what I am given. It is called stewardship not ownership. We will come back to these issues too.

Suffice it to say that any of you who like to be in control of anyone or anything are in ownership not stewardship. You will find the *'me and mine'* words not far from your lips if you are honest.

We may love to give freely and be seen to be generous, but the purpose of giving is not to feel good, it is to invest our time, money and lives in the Kingdom in the way in which the King directs.

Money is only one currency we have. Time is our most valuable currency, but more about that later too.

It is important to God that we grow up into maturity in order that He can trust us with the Kingdom.

Use or misuse of our 'treasure', whether that be great or small, contributes to our alignment with Him, and therefore our growth and suitability for reigning and ruling in this life and the next.

SECTION 2

Making a start

Now is this not a happy business? Christ, the rich, noble and holy bridegroom, takes in marriage this poor, contemptible and sinful little prostitute; takes away all of her evil, and bestows all His goodness upon her! It is no longer possible for sin to overwhelm her, for she is now found in Christ and is swallowed up by Him so that she possesses a rich righteousness in her bridegroom.

Martin Luther[1]

1

Making a start

As I sought the Lord for this chapter, I was impressed that we do not need more information but we need revelation: not perspiration (effort) but inspiration. That we need to know how to do this thing because we know very well what we are not, but how to become what we ought to be, that is the burning question for us.

He said to me two things:

1. *'I never ask you to do something without giving you the means to do it'.*
2. *'What I ask is therefore totally possible for you'.*

Paul sums it up for us:

Torn Between One Way and Another

I can anticipate the response that is coming: "I know that all God's commands are spiritual, but I'm not. Isn't this also your experience?" Yes. I'm full of myself – after all, I've spent a long time in sin's prison. What I don't understand about myself is that I decide one way, but then I act another, doing things I absolutely despise. So if I can't be trusted to figure out what is best for myself and then do it, it becomes obvious that God's command is necessary.

But I need something more! For if I know the law but still can't keep it, and if the power of sin within me keeps sabotaging my best intentions, I obviously need help! I realise that I don't have what it takes. I can will it, but I can't do it. I decide to do good, but I don't really do it; I decide not to do bad, but then I do it anyway. My decisions, such as they are, don't result in actions. Something has gone wrong deep within me and gets the better of me every time.

It happens so regularly that it's predictable. The moment I decide to do good, sin is there to trip me up. I truly delight in God's commands, but it's pretty obvious that not all of me joins in that delight. Parts of me covertly rebel, and just when I least expect it, they take charge.

I've tried everything and nothing helps. I'm at the end of my rope. Is there no one who can do anything for me? Isn't that the real question? The answer, thank God, is that Jesus Christ can and does. He acted to set things right in this life of contradictions where I want to serve God with all my heart and mind, but am pulled by the influence of sin to do something totally different. (Romans 7:14-25 MSG).

How about *Be perfect as your heavenly Father is perfect?* (Matthew 5:48).

What?! I can hear the indrawn breath, that is impossible! But He said it.

He said it to Abram too (Genesis 17:1).

Maybe, just maybe, we have an erroneous understanding of the word *'perfect'*. It literally means, to grow up, mature.

It must be possible to do this thing, but maybe not from our perspective right now. But our reach must exceed our grasp or we will not grow.

Note
1. www.thegospelcoalition.org quoted in Alister E. McGrath, Christian Spirituality: An Introduction (Oxford, 1999), pages 158-159.

2

Crisis to process

Do you remember I said the view from the penthouse was going to be different from the view from the basement?

This thing is about a journey into the heart of God for you. Where you go from one place to another, from crisis to process and from living life from an earth-bound perspective to living from a higher place.

You are now seated in heavenly places in Christ.

That is why Jesus can ask the things we see in the Sermon on the Mount of you and expect that you to do them. He can say, *'be perfect as your Heavenly Father is perfect'*, and expect you to comply.

But it causes something. It's called a crisis, from which we move to process.

Jesus holds out to us how He sees us and we are plunged into a crisis.

He sees a mature bride; mature in *His* love, mature in agape.

The difference is in the **type** of love. It is no longer *natural* love, but His, divine love, the love of choice; received, (1 John 4:19) then lived out.

She's prepared for her wedding; longing for her bridegroom and watching waiting for His appearing...

You, as the bride, are in a time of preparation and you are going from crisis to process. You are being matured in love, His love.

Just as a natural bride would be excited about her wedding day, so He wants to impart to you the excitement He feels about the forthcoming union, so that you may be excited also.

He is excited, ecstatic that He is getting you for a bride for eternity. You are the *'joy that was set before Him'* (Hebrews 12:2) when He endured the cross. You are going to reign and rule with Him.

He is not deterred by your feelings of unworthiness or inability because He has made you worthy and able, what needs to happen now is that you fully walk into everything He has already made possible for you.

By faith. You know what faith is:

> *the substance of things hoped for, the evidence of things not seen...* (Hebrews 11:1).

The key is that you understand who you now are, and where you have been placed.

- You are a new creation, in the Christ.
- You are seated in heavenly places, in Him.
- Your old life no longer exists.
- Your old values no longer exist.
- You are in the School of the Spirit.
- Your decision-making is now based on what God is saying, not on what you think…
- Feelings are going to take a back seat.
- Faith is going to rise.
- You have everything you need; you are clothed in His righteousness.

We can do this. Make sure you have the right shoes on, something sturdy, there will be some detours and mountains to climb on the way. Take my hand, let's go!

3

Two lists

These lists are about one little word really. That word is *desire*.

Ooops! I bet you thought we were not supposed to speak about such things.

That is because we usually connect desire with things sexual or at least physical. If it is me then it is the self-indulgence of an iced bun!

Or things we would say we 'lust' over. Now there's another word we need to look at. Let's say it together and get it over, all together now – *LUST!*

That's torn it, now it is out in the open. We cannot deal with something if we deny its existence, can we? If we think we shouldn't have desires, we are in for problems because we cannot deny them.

What shall we say then? Is the law sin? Certainly not! On the contrary, I would not have known sin except through the law. For I would not have known covetousness unless the law had said, "You shall not covet." (Romans 7:7).

'Covetousness', lust, longing, acquisitiveness, desire –
brilliant Paul, on the nail as ever, pointing out that the law
and the commandments were there to show us that we had
something innately wrong with us, something deep inside that
we could do absolutely nothing about and which we would do
well to recognise – the old sin nature.

We would not have known what the lust of the flesh, the lust
of the eye or the pride of life were about without the law.

Now we are in knowledge, we have the information; what we
need now is *revelation* on how to walk free of this prison we
were born into.

Well, thanks be to God in Christ Jesus is the answer. He has
given us all we need for a life of godliness, hear Peter on the
subject now:

Fruitful Growth in the Faith

> *But also for this very reason, giving all diligence, add to
> your faith virtue, to virtue knowledge, to knowledge self-
> control, to self-control perseverance, to perseverance
> godliness, to godliness brotherly kindness, and to
> brotherly kindness love. For if these things are yours
> and abound, you will be neither barren nor unfruitful in
> the knowledge of our Lord Jesus Christ. For he who
> lacks these things is shortsighted, even to blindness,
> and has forgotten that he was cleansed from his old
> sins.* (2 Peter 1:5-9)

It seems to me that it is all about remembering what we

have been cleansed from; beating the old habit patterns and staying where we have been put, in Christ.

Living from there, as my dear young friend Gregory said when he told us about heaven. Let me remind you what he said:

"You know Who has spent forever in the Kingdom, and is accustomed to its culture? Jesus. So our new self, who is in Him, is the genius that already knows how to act like a citizen of Heaven!

Live in and through the new self and we will be ready."

That will be it then.

Next time we really will take a look at those two lists. We can do this thing.

4

Desire and the two lists

I need to explore this word desire.

> *"You shall have no other gods before Me.*
> *You shall not make for yourself a carved image.*
> *You shall not take the name of the Lord your God in vain.*
> *Observe the Sabbath day, to keep it holy.*
> *Honour your father and your mother.*
> *You shall not murder.*
> *You shall not commit adultery.*
> *You shall not steal.*
> *You shall not bear false witness against your neighbour.*
> *You shall not covet."* (Exodus 20:3-17).

I hear you say *'Oh, it's the Ten Commandments I know those…'* Four towards God and six towards those around us.

"Yes, I know". God has not done away with them either. *"Oh! I thought we were under grace…"*

We are, but, we do not have to look very closely to see that *desire* is linked to every one of them; you could add *'to get what you want'* after each one starting with the first, *'don't make yourself another god – to get what you want...'* Get the drift?

The only exception is the fourth one, but I don't know though. If I pray enough, do enough, read the bible enough, perspiration... don't let's go there.

Early in my Christian walk I got caught up in legalism – it is not difficult in a Pentecostal environment. I thought *'coarse jesting'* was laughing a lot! I soon found how wrong I was and everyone around me got happy as a result.

But there is a list of things Paul mentions in two places: 1 Corinthians 6 and Galatians 5, that preclude us *inheriting* the Kingdom. In other words, seeing His Kingdom come in our lives, which indicate that the King is *reigning* in us governing how we live.

These things will not affect our salvation, but they will affect the extent to which Jesus has the *rule* in our life if they are allowed to remain there.

Merging the two lists they look like this:

Fornication, idolatry, adultery, effeminacy, homosexuality; stealing, coveting, getting drunk; reviling, swindling, being immoral, or impure, practicing sorcery; enmity, strife and jealousy, anger, disputing, dissension, factions, envy and carousing, filthiness, silly talk and coarse jesting and the like.

All these are *behavioural* issues and they underline the fact that Jesus is not Lord in those areas, because if He was, we would not be *doing* these things. Persistence in them prevents us from receiving the Kingdom as an inheritance.

They are about character and conduct. The second comes out of the first.

What is being spoken about here is not something where we slipped up once or twice. It would be legalism to imply that and if that were the case none of us would qualify for the inheritance! No, this is a persistent, insistent, wilful, cold blooded, dare I say *rebellious* decision, to live our lives in a way that gives us what we want. It satisfies our *desire* for our lives, and it is usually, *physical* and it precludes us *inheriting* the Kingdom.

I have no axe to grind either way beloved about any of these behaviours, but I do have a duty of care to point these things out. Physical gratification is a heavy price to pay if it costs us our inheritance.

It costs us because we are doing a trade; trading whatever our particular physical need is for an eternal Kingdom. We are trading the eternal for the temporal, just like Esau whose god was his belly as Paul would say.

But it is your life.

As long as we are ruled by our desires we cannot walk in the freedom and intent of the Kingdom.

You get to choose.

There's no condemnation, no judgement for those who are 'in Christ'. What there is, is a loss of freedom in this life and to an extent your eternal reward.

But again, you choose whether you live in bondage or freedom, entirely up to you.

But it was for freedom and Christ set you free.

Freedom from the dominion of the self-centred life.

5

Discipline and desire produce delight

Someone coined the phrase *'when discipline and desire get married, they produce delight'.*

This is certainly the truth for us, when we bring our lives under the joyful Lordship of Christ *and* discipline ourselves (otherwise known as self-control) there is a marriage made in heaven which produces delight in our lives and in the lives of those around us.

We are life changers and atmosphere changers.

Faith levels rise when we are around. All things are possible when we are around. Heaven comes down when we are around.

So what we desire here is important.

The Heritage of the Righteous and the Calamity of the Wicked

Do not fret because of evildoers,
Nor be envious of the workers of iniquity.
For they shall soon be cut down like the grass,
And wither as the green herb.
Trust in the Lord, and do good;
Dwell in the land, and feed on His faithfulness.
Delight yourself also in the Lord,
And He shall give you the desires of your heart. (Psalm 37:1-4)

The heritage of the righteous (the inheritance of the righteous). Here we are again, right back to the inheritance issue.

We are prone, as my mother would say, to *'cut off our noses to spite our faces.'* In other words, we do the silliest things that actually harm us; and that with our eyes wide open.

Fatally flawed we are.

There is only one place from which to live in safety and that is where He has put us, in Christ. There, double wrapped in the Father and the Son, we are safely carried and nurtured by the Holy Spirit into everything He has for us.

We are alive and free.

Except for one thing. Free will. A name for nothing someone else once said.

Our will is only free to step *away* from God, once we are in Christ. Before that it was free to pursue Satan's plan, until we chose otherwise.

Out from his dominion you find you do have a will and it is like a chain around your neck, constantly pulling you away from the Love of your life back into bondage – the man in the prison cell we spoke about in the last series, comfortable in his bondage.

No wonder Jesus taught us to pray *"Thy will be done, Thy Kingdom come…"*

We do not seem to have come very far yet, do we?

6

Enlargement

Hear me when I call, O God of my righteousness: thou hast enlarged me when I was in distress; have mercy upon me, and hear my prayer. (Psalm 4:1 KJV).

And of His fulness have we all received (John 1:16)

We all want the fulness, which means of necessity enlargement, but we do not all want what goes with it. Distress.

Enlargement = distress. For every step of enlargement you take, there will be two things: conflict and distress.

We want to be developed, and enlarged but painlessly, please!

'There is no other stream'.

We are right back to fact that the truth when it first comes displaces everything we thought we knew, and elicits a less than positive reaction from us.

Plainly, we do not like it. We need a change of lens but we do not like the process.

God's purpose in disturbing our nest is that we might get bigger; grow on the inside; make room for more of Him; Thy Kingdom come.

And the way He does it is through allowing conflict, difficulty and distress in our lives.

You know, somehow, we just do not hear Him. The soft voice doesn't penetrate. But circumstances do; pain gets your attention, fast.

He does not cause the circumstances, but He does use them. In His wisdom He allows what He could easily prevent by His power.

When He comes to us with more of Himself, we present our little box marked 'church' all neat and tidy and expect Him to fit His Kingdom into that.

Beloved, it will not fit.

When He comes He always brings something bigger than you currently have and if you try to squeeze the new into the old you will have to cut the edges to squeeze it in and you run the risk of losing everything.

Nope.

Like Neo, you remember him, the guy in the Matrix who was

offered a blue or a red pill, he chose the red one and promptly began to see things completely differently from the way he had seen them before. We need a different way of seeing things; we need a red pill.

If you see it as a parable, you could say Neo came out of the kingdom of darkness and saw everything in glorious light and technicolour.

With us this is incremental. God does not give us everything at once in pill form. He works little by little but He keeps coming back with more.

We go from crisis to process, remember?

You can never have too much of a good thing, can you? Or can you?

Sometimes what He comes with does not taste too palatable; it cuts across everything we have understood and are comfortable with. Remember the guy in the prison cell he called home; he didn't want to move at first either, he was so happy in his bondage.

At first we refuse the wide-open space and freedom that the Kingdom holds out.

It is for freedom that Christ has set us free. (Galatians 5:1).

Back to Peter and the sheet was let down three times before he got the message. He was discomforted big time. What

God was asking went against everything he had been taught, not some things, everything. But he did move his feet the third time.

Do not think that God will not keep coming back until you move your feet, because He will. He will not be put off. He will just keep coming back with the same thing until you get it, really, get it, and move.

By then you find yourself enlarged, uncomfortable; learning a new language and a new way of relating to everyone and everything around you.

Normal life in the Kingdom.

Distress and development beloved of God, go together.

7

The time is now

Thirty years ago, the Lord said to me *'The mantle that was on him is now upon you'.*

He was referring to a teacher under whose ministry I had sat for some years and his mantle to teach had been removed and given to me.

The way it happened was this. He had been challenged by God. *'The cost'*, he said, *'was too great.'* I watched as the fellowship got smaller and smaller. Eventually the church closed and he moved away

Ichabod – *'the glory has departed'* – was written over the door. (1 Samuel 4:21).

This may come as a shock to you, but it is possible to lose the call and the spiritual He gift bestowed upon us if we lose momentum and cease to walk in step with the Spirit. If we drop out of the race.

He steps in and removes the gift; it was His in the first place, and He takes it back. When He does, the light goes out.

Don't believe me?

> *Nevertheless I have this against you, that you have left your first love. Remember therefore from where you have fallen; repent and do the first works, or else I will come to you quickly and remove your lamp-stand from its place – unless you repent.* (Revelation 2:4-5 Ephesus)

Ephesus commended for its works and discernment here, but the thing God had against it was that it had left its first love. Walked away. Honeymoon over, love cooled. She just did not love Him anymore.

How it works out is that the things of the earth and this life become more important to us than God Himself and the advancement of the Kingdom in our lives; husband, wife, children, job, people, friends, money, possessions, position, power or the cares of the world and the *'deceitfulness of riches'* as the Bible calls them. All spoil the crop.

Nothing wrong with any of these provided they do not have you and you have them. When they exert more influence over you than He does, it will negatively affect something.

In this case it was the person's gifting and ability to lead others into the truth, their mantle, that was removed. He continued to teach, but it was lifeless; the word without the Spirit. The ways of God, past finding out.

This is not, I emphasise, about loss of salvation, but loss of usefulness in the Kingdom.

I have known other instances, too, where the light of the Spirit has been removed. God is not capricious, He really does not change His mind but we can disqualify ourselves. We lose our usefulness by our own deliberate choices.

Before you ask 'what about Romans 11 then?', he is not talking about the spiritual gifts here:

> *For the gifts and the calling of God are irrevocable.* (Romans 11:29)

In context this passage refers to Israel and the covenants and promises He made to them.

Why am I telling you this? When He calls us into something He is serious about it and wants us to take it seriously too, this is Kingdom business.

There are no casual friends in the Kingdom. It is not how you start but how you finish:

> *I don't know about you, but I'm running hard for the finish line. I'm giving it everything I've got. No sloppy living for me! I'm staying alert and in top condition. I'm not going to get caught napping, telling everyone else all about it and then missing out myself.* (1 Corinthians 9:26-27 MSG)

Paul takes the analogy of a runner in a race, and speaks of going for it as after the prize. He constantly referred to the Christian journey as a race, to which we need to apply ourselves.

God is serious about His Kingdom coming in our lives. Let's face it, we keep asking for it! *'Thy Kingdom come.'* We ask for it all the time.

Sooner or later He is going to give us what we are asking for. But it will not look as we thought. Because of this there will be challenges along the way to lose more and more of ourselves and the things we hold dear in this life, so we can receive more of Him.

If there is a call on your life you will do well to protect it by making the right choices when the time comes, by putting the King and His Kingdom first, or you may find yourself being disqualified too. Disqualified means ordered to stand aside – not rejected – so someone else gets the crown that was intended for you; the one God wanted *you* to have but your choices, or lack of them, have disqualified you.

> *And everyone who competes for the prize is temperate in all things. Now they do it to obtain a perishable crown, but we for an imperishable crown. Therefore I run thus: not with uncertainty. Thus I fight: not as one who beats the air. But I discipline my body and bring it into subjection, lest, when I have preached to others, I myself should become disqualified.* (1 Corinthians 9:25-27)

God never, ever changes and in these coming days and months we will be seeing a different face of our Lord and Saviour as the battle of the universe nears its end and He presents Himself as Jehovah Sabaoth – the Coming Warrior King.

There is going to be a collision of light and darkness the like of which the world has never seen before Jesus comes again.

Now is the time to make the decision on where you are going to be placing your feet. Time to get ready; to save wasting time trying to get ready when the time comes.

Time to start taking this thing more seriously than just a ticket to heaven?

8

Freedom – the ability to stop and start

Freedom in any area of our lives can be described as the ability to start and stop. Once we have the ability to stop something having started it, we are some way to self-control.

For instance, it has taken a long time for me to be able to have one biscuit or one chocolate and not polish off the whole packet or box.

Bob Mumford is quoted as saying someone spoke to him about his appetite thus: *'Bob, the Lord spent years putting stuff into you, please do not destroy it with a fork'.*

Right where the rubber hits the road. Self-control is really all about this. Freedom is being able to control your fork!

And another part of your mouth – your tongue. Being able to stop and start. To listen twice as much as you speak. Two ears, one mouth!

You may have a problem with talking too much – you need

to apply the ability to stop once in a while; take a look at the faces of the people who are being subjected to your incessant chatter because you like to talk.

Just a thought, basic stuff, but this is what this part of the book is about. It is practical. Right where we live. The little things.

Things that are so much a part of us that we really do not notice them until there is that persistent voice saying *'We need to take a look at this'*. We ignore it at our peril.

The Kingdom really is within you. And it is coming – fast.

Take a look at what Jesus' brother said about the mouth and the tongue particularly:

Taming the tongue

Not many of you should become teachers, my fellow believers, because you know that we who teach will be judged more strictly. We all stumble in many ways. Anyone who is never at fault in what they say is perfect, able to keep their whole body in check.

When we put bits into the mouths of horses to make them obey us, we can turn the whole animal. Or take ships as an example. Although they are so large and are driven by strong winds, they are steered by a very small rudder wherever the pilot wants to go. Likewise, the tongue is a small part of the body, but it makes great boasts. Consider what a great forest is set on fire by a small spark. The tongue also is a fire, a world of evil among the parts of the body. It corrupts the whole body, sets the whole course of one's life on fire, and is itself set on fire by hell.

All kinds of animals, birds, reptiles and sea creatures are being tamed and have been tamed by mankind, but no human being can tame the tongue. It is a restless evil, full of deadly poison.

With the tongue we praise our Lord and Father, and with it we curse human beings, who have been made in God's likeness. Out of the same mouth come praise and cursing. My brothers and sisters, this should not be. Can both fresh water and salt water flow from the same spring? My brothers and sisters, can a fig-tree bear olives, or a grapevine bear figs? Neither can a salt spring produce fresh water. (James 3: 3-12 NIV)

I think I will let the word do its work.

9

Making it real

One of the things He loves to do is make what He has taught us real in our experience.

You will read a teaching like this and then you will have an encounter with Him, and an experience as He shows you the reality of what it means.

The pressure comes – through circumstances, people, things, worry. It is at this point you come to understand we give Him in a time of peace what He extracts in a time of war.

He will come to you in the circumstance or whatever; woo your heart, reveal His Majesty, and cause you to bow in worship before Him; acknowledging He is your Lord and you are His love slave as once again you come into surrender.

All this is not difficult unless we make it so. When He comes and shows us Himself, He breaks our heart with His tenderness and beauty, and we realise what we are like without Him and how much we need to be changed from the inside out.

Beryl Moore

We come to see that we can joyously say with Paul *'in me dwells no good thing'* (Romans 7:18) and we can say it without regret because by our placement in Him; we can be all He asks of us.

It is called revelation not perspiration. Effort has no part, grace is all. He loves revealing Himself. He does it from Genesis to Revelation. It is progressive.

He loves showing us more and more of His beauty, Majesty and grace, in order that we may become like Him.

What we behold, we will become. If we behold Majesty, we will become like Him. Our character will change. We soften and become mouldable, teachable and pliable. All those lovely things.

We find the joy of repentance. Repentance, having another thought, will become a way of life, because the thought you had yesterday, won't do for today.

He just got bigger. You just got more like Him.

Encounter. Beholding. Becoming. Brilliant.

How is it working out for you?

10

The prayer of relinquishment

There is the 'Lordship prayer' as I call it, and then there is this one, the prayer of relinquishment.

I read this in a book on prayer by Catherine Marshall but then I adapted it and made it my own. Right at the end she quotes a prayer of a missionary who had prayed for many, many, years for the Lord's healing which did not come; it went something like this:

'Lord, I have tried to get you to heal me in the way I want for years.

Right now I give up. I relinquish my demands.

I have come to the end of demanding from You what I want, in the way I want it, when I want it, and I simply ask that You will have your way in my life, whatever that way may be, from this moment on.

I surrender.' [1]

That is quite a place to come to if you think about it.

This dear one had obviously stormed heaven's gates for years, and finally exhausted, had given up and expressed the words *'Thy Kingdom come'* in a different way.

It is amazing to me that we have come seemingly so far and yet here we still are, talking about the 'Lord's Prayer' that we pray so often.

The Kingdom is about displacement. His life for yours. His will for yours.

There is no in between if you are to have abundant life, fulness. Jesus said:

"I have come that you might have life, and have it to the full." (John 10:10).

Abundance. Fulness.

I wonder with our self-seeking world-view just what we thought He meant? Let me take a guess – money, houses, cars, holidays, and job satisfaction?

You get that, we are told, if we seek the *Kingdom* first:

"But seek first the kingdom of God and His righteousness, and all these things shall be added to you." (Matthew 6:33 KJV).

He was talking to His followers, believers and disciples. Ooops.

We are out of alignment again somewhere. Time for a mid-course correction.

Note
1. 'Adventures in Prayer', p 81 Catherine Marshall, Hodder and Stoughton 1975

11

Change in the wind

When there is a change in the wind, in sailing parlance they would shout *"mind the boom"*.

If the boom swings as the boat turns in an effort to catch the wind, you can get a whack on the back of the head and be unceremoniously dunked in cold water.

This little bite-sized piece is about what happens when God makes a mid-course correction to your little craft, or His church, in other words when there is a change in the wind.

Yachtsmen will talk about tacking. What they mean is that because they are subject to the wind they must make zigzag movements as they travel towards their destination.

They cannot go in a straight line because they are subject to the wind and so they have to catch the wind – which is where *"mind the boom"* comes in.

When the boat turns and a sea is running, we need to be quick to keep with it or we may find ourselves over the side.

We need to be able to move and adapt quickly to the new direction.

When God makes a mid-course correction in His church it is exactly the same. You need to move and quick.

And mind your head. He is about to mess with it! He offends it, your head that is, to get to your heart. Always.

He turns over all our well thought through ideas of what He means and where He is headed and indeed, where our life was headed.

The old saying *'if you want to make God laugh, tell Him your plans'* would fit well here.

If the Spirit turns our boat and we don't turn with Him, personally or corporately, we will only have one direction left to travel in, over the side, in other words the flesh.

If we are not moving in and with the Spirit of God, that is the only alternative. Everything will become very difficult. (Galatians 3:1-3).

When we miss Him like this, we are without direction. It does not matter how far we travel. If we are headed in the wrong direction we won't reach our destination.

Re-adjusting and re-orienting ourselves to the new perspective in the Spirit can be painful, prolonged and difficult, but in order to keep the vessel on course we must continually *"come about"* and make those mid-course corrections.

How long it will take is governed by our response time. This applies both to us as individuals and corporately as church groups. Right now, there is a change in the wind. The emphasis of the Spirit has changed.

Is there any mid-course correction that the Spirit is impressing on you? Do you need to speed up your response time?

Time to turn about, duck, or you may find yourself overboard.

God does not consult when He makes a change of direction. It is called Majesty. Beautiful, brilliant, Majesty.

His Majesty. King Jesus.

12

Flexibility and pliability

If we are to contain the new wine of the Kingdom we will need to learn to be pliable. Flexible, mobile, supple, agile, elastic, yielding. Willing to change.

Contrast with inflexible: brittle, stiff, hard, unbending, rigid, intractable. We have all met people who come into the latter category.

How do we shape up? Honesty test coming up.

Let us lay the canon of scripture down and measure ourselves – there may be some stretching coming:

Love Your Enemies
"Here's another old saying that deserves a second look: 'Eye for eye, tooth for tooth.' Is that going to get us anywhere? Here's what I propose: 'Don't hit back at all.' If someone strikes you, stand there and take it. If someone drags you into court and sues for the shirt off your back, gift-wrap your best coat and make a present of it. And if someone takes unfair advantage of you, use the occasion to practice the servant life. No more

tit-for-tat stuff. Live generously." (Matthew 5:38-42 MSG)

This really upsets the fruit basket!

Turn the other cheek; go the extra mile; if they take you for all you have, give them what you are wearing; live generously.

The boat just turned about and we very nearly got hit by the boom!

The law of the Kingdom of Love in action. Right where we live. Right where it hurts.

Don't hit back. Do not retaliate. Give them all you have if they want it without trying to recover anything. Right in the pocketbook.

God takes us from one situation to another to teach us His ways – the ways in which He wants us to live as Kingdom citizens.

Let's clear up the first part of this, the *'eye for an eye'* bit. This was a restraint order not a licence to harm.

It was designed to stop them taking more from one another, in the case of a perceived wrong than the Lord intended, so He put limits on their retaliation; their pay back.

Now He says, you have heard it said *'get back to the extent that you have lost but not more'* but now I say to you… and He promptly unfolds His heart in the issue

Don't try to get anything back. Don't seek to recompense for evil. Don't do it.

What! I can hear the screech, *'a pound of flesh...'*

May I remind you of the unmerciful servant who had been forgiven so much and then went out and beat his servant within an inch of his life; he was handed over to the tormentors!

We are going to need a lot more flexibility to live this Kingdom lifestyle. We need to be *s-t-r-e-t-c-h-e-d.* Some to contain this wine.

And it starts here.

How do you react, or respond, when you are attacked, robbed, asked to go further than you want in a situation? Or reviled and cursed, your good spoken ill of? How do you react?

I think we need to spend some time unpicking this one or we are in danger of being superficial about what is really being asked of us, as we come under the joyful discipline of living a Kingdom lifestyle in the Kingdom where love is the key. His Kingdom really does come in us and through us.

13

Retaliation

I can distinctly remember when I learned, and was shocked by, my desire to retaliate.

I had a kitten, tiny little thing, and it scratched me. My response was to raise my hand to smack it – hard. I was horrified, this little scrap was about to feel the full force of *my* paw, I could have knocked it silly.

By God's grace I never made contact. But the lesson I learned stayed with me.

I looked inside myself and saw that when push came to shove I would instantly and instinctively, hit back, and I was not about to pull my punches. *'If you hurt me, I'll make sure you get double back pal'.*

Now, in every circumstance when I am provoked, I remember how quickly my flesh rose and I wanted to give that pussycat a bunch of five-fold ministry!

It has caused me to get that reaction under control so that I respond, rather than react, in circumstances where

I am under pressure.

Retaliation is a natural *reaction,* not a spiritual *response.* It often extracts double or even triple for the perceived offence.

As I said in the last chapter, the *'eye for an eye'* command was about damage limitation not payback.

It was a protection for the one being injured as well as the restraint needed towards the offender. Like the laws on divorce, it was permitted because of their hardness of heart. Hardness of heart.

This is why He had to give us a new heart, the old one was hard. He expects us to live from there, not from the natural, but the new supernatural heart within us.

We have a new seed within which is capable of responding to a higher law than the law of retaliation.

It contains the royal law of Love. It keeps no record of wrong. Does not repay evil for evil. It is patient. Kind. Not self-absorbed.

It puts up with anything and everything. It trusts, hopes and endures, no matter what. You can find a list in 1 Corinthians 13.

How is it working out for you?

14

Revenge

'Revenge is a dish best served cold,' said Marlon Brando in 'The Godfather'.

Revenge. One of the most basic instincts of the fallen human condition. *"You just wait, I'll get you back for that".*

A dish best served cold. *'Let me enjoy the thought of what I intend to do to get even with you'.*

What does Jesus have to say? *"Here's what I propose: Don't hit back at all. If someone strikes you, stand there and take it."*

That is not what we had in mind, most of us, that is. So why would the Lord allow such a thing to happen, that someone slapped us? To show what is inside, that's why.

Resentment, rebellion, revenge, retaliation. I will get you, pay back double...

He knows just how to push our buttons to get those ungodly reactions to surface. How kind is that?

When they surface we get the opportunity to face and acknowledge them and get free! That is kind.

No condemnation.

We cannot get free from something we will not admit we have.

Time to 'fess up' then. Just what ungodly reactions do you need to admit to?

Wouldn't that be nice to be set free from that desire – oooh it is that word again – to avenge yourself; to pay back like for like or even give a bit more for good measure.

Who *really* needs to turn the other cheek? The one who wants revenge is the answer.

He wants to set us free. Let us look at how Jesus and Paul dealt with it:

> *When Jesus said this, one of the officials near by slapped him in the face. "Is this the way you answer the high priest?" he demanded. "If I said something wrong," Jesus replied, "testify as to what is wrong. But if I spoke the truth, why did you strike me?" (John 18:22-23 NIV)*

No revenge there. Why didn't Jesus react? There was nothing in Him. No resentment, no revenge, no rebellion, no retaliation, no desire to get even. He was without sin.

What about Paul then? He was a man:

Paul looked straight at the Sanhedrin and said, 'My brothers, I have fulfilled my duty to God in all good conscience to this day.' At this the high priest Ananias ordered those standing near Paul to strike him on the mouth. Then Paul said to him, 'God will strike you, you whitewashed wall! You sit there to judge me according to the law, yet you yourself violate the law by commanding that I be struck!' Those who were standing near Paul said, 'How dare you insult God's high priest!' Paul replied, 'Brothers, I did not realise that he was the high priest; for it is written: "Do not speak evil about the ruler of your people." (Acts 23:1-5 NIV)

In the first instance, though his response was straight, it was not uttered with a wrong attitude, and the second time, he apologised!

Attitude we will find in the Kingdom, is all important because it determines altitude.

More to come.

15

Live generously

Live generously. (Matthew 5:42 MSG)

The Kingdom is not about rules, and yet it is. We need rules or we would have no boundaries; Jesus didn't come to do away with the Law but to write it on our hearts.

Keep in mind those ten commandments if you will.
One of the little rules is in Matthew 5:42, the Message says it well in two words: *"live generously"*.

Didn't I said that God loves to make things real in our experience?

While I was preparing this and thinking and praying about the content, I found a pen. Nothing special, just an ordinary stick biro. But it flowed beautifully.

I don't know where it came from, but I found it. And I liked it. I appropriated it. I put it in a box near my chair, where I could get at it and keep an eye on it.

Good. Mine. Ownership. Pleasure.

Then someone came to do some work for me and suddenly, here is *my* pen being held aloft and the exclamation: *"This is a lovely pen, it writes beautifully, can I have it?"*

S'mine… I nearly got hit with that boom! I had to move fast. I saw the Holy Spirit's grin – *'here it is, giving, freely, what are you going to do? You can't teach it without living it…'*

I laughed. *"Of course you can, go ahead".* Later I bought a packet!

But I am free, you can have as many pens as you like, they don't have me, I have them.

He will *always* make it real in our experience. A little test, but a significant one.

Daily you will be faced up with such little (or larger) tests of whether or not you are going to put what He is showing you about Kingdom living into practice.

Stop there and think about it for a moment. Just how is it working out for you?

16

That Shrinking Feeling

In Acts 20:27, Paul is about to leave and he says something very interesting:

for I did not shrink from declaring to you the whole counsel of God.

There can be a shrinking feeling for anyone who is called to declare the *whole* counsel of God, not just the bits that people find acceptable; likewise, for those who hear the message...

This is why I say that when the truth first comes it is almost always received negatively. We don't like it and we rise up against it.

For instance, someone was offended recently when I said there is no second chance after death. They had lost a loved one and wanted to think the person has another chance; sad. But no matter what you might like to think and comfort yourself with, there is no opportunity to change our mind about Jesus after death. The scripture is clear:

it is appointed for men to die once, but after this the judgment (Hebrews 9:27)

We do not like being faced up with the truth of our behaviours and what we are involved in, or having our belief systems challenged.

The word when it comes by the Spirit has a way of cutting through all our carefully constructed defence mechanisms and rendering us naked as the day that we were born.

For the word of God is alive and active. Sharper than any double-edged sword, it penetrates even to dividing soul and spirit, joints and marrow; it judges the thoughts and attitudes of the heart. (Hebrews 4:12)

The thoughts and attitudes of the heart. It is at this point we have a choice. To make that mid-course correction and keep our momentum going or stay where we are.

For the person I mentioned earlier the boom hit them on the head and messed with it. They went over the side of the boat. What I said and the scripture said, did not line up with what they wanted to believe.

We began by talking about Majesty, and it is time we reminded ourselves that when Jesus comes again it will not be as a helpless babe in a manger, but as the conquering Hero; the Warrior King to separate His sheep from the goats and to take control over His Kingdom once and for all.

It is time we stopped making excuses for Him and softening

what He says. Time we stopped trying to domesticate the Lion of Judah.

This is His time and His season. As Jesus presents Himself to His church, His Bride, in these days, she will find herself unable to resist His advances. She will indeed come to the place described in Revelation 22:17:

The Spirit and the bride say, "Come".

This is showing us that the Bride has become mature enough to desire Him and to cry out for His coming. It shows us too that the Holy Spirit's work is complete in her, so in unity they can cry *'Come'*:

His response?

"Surely I am coming quickly."
Amen.
Even so, come, Lord Jesus! (Revelation 22:20)

We have a bit of a way to go before we are united with Him, in crying for His return and *'longing for His appearing.'* (2 Timothy 4:8).

We need to put on our running shoes and narrow the gap between where He stands and where we are right now. I will not shrink from proclaiming to you the whole counsel of God which may mean we have to brush up on our sailing skills and learn how to duck as that boom swings over our heads, or it will really get messed with.

When I really begin to get in to teaching the Sermon on the Mount as Jesus intended, it will mess with your head, your heart and probably your pocketbook; your time and everything else as well.

But it is all good.

I just felt I should remind you of those two things: His Majesty and His ability to mess with your head.

17

Whoever has ears to hear

Jesus, in His humanity, only ever did what pleased the Father.

Question: Is that in your thinking to only do what pleases the Father?

If it isn't may I suggest that you stop right there and take a little time to consider the question.

Pleasing the Father may change your life completely. You could experience radical renewal rather than business as usual. The Kingdom could come inside you in its fulness.

It is entirely up to you but from this point on we are going to look at what pleases *Him.*

What gives Him joy. What satisfies Him. What glorifies Him. What magnifies Him.

Jesus, it was said, would *'see the travail of His soul and be satisfied'.* (Isaiah 53:11). I want that more than anything. Do you?

No man building a tower does not sit down and count the cost first. This could turn out to be a cost counting exercise. It will cost you in terms of time, money, friends, family, possessions, pastimes and hobbies.

But no-man leaves mother, father, sister, brother, houses land in this life and does not receive an abundance of all these in the service of the King

"Suppose one of you wants to build a tower. Won't you first sit down and estimate the cost to see if you have enough money to complete it? For if you lay the foundation and are not able to finish it, everyone who sees it will ridicule you, saying, 'This person began to build and wasn't able to finish.'

"Or suppose a king is about to go to war against another king. Won't he first sit down and consider whether he is able with ten thousand men to oppose the one coming against him with twenty thousand? If he is not able, he will send a delegation while the other is still a long way off and will ask for terms of peace. In the same way, those of you who do not give up everything you have cannot be my disciples.

"Salt is good, but if it loses its saltiness, how can it be made salty again? It is fit neither for the soil nor for the manure pile; it is thrown out.

"Whoever has ears to hear, let them hear." (Luke 14:28-35 NIV)

Funny that, *"Whoever has ears to hear, let them hear"*. It is almost the same thing Jesus says to the churches in Revelation.

Full counsel of God coming up!

18

Inheritance

Something that is really bugging me right now is the subject of our inheritance. Both in this life, and the life to come.

Jesus and Paul both spoke about it. To inherit something is to come into something unearned. We have not worked for it, like receiving a wage or salary.

But we need to have a certain kind of lens to see it. I want to explore just a couple of things about it.

The first and probably most important is that there is a cost to receiving and walking in it, and most often it has to do with attitudes and behaviour.

Our inheritance can be lost or traded through our behaviour. God is not a withholder, but He does have certain requirements of us. He created us as moral beings and He is restoring that virtue to us. We cannot use the liberty we have in the Christ as an occasion to sin. Please understand, He is not consumed with sin but with inheritance. He wants us to inherit.

We have to get topsides of the old man and live in the new,

because it is in the new man we find our inheritance.

A corpse is beyond inheriting anything; you remember the corpse of course, we spoke about it before.

> *Indeed, I have been crucified with Christ. My ego is no longer central. It is no longer important that I appear righteous before you or have your good opinion, and I am no longer driven to impress God. Christ lives in me. The life you see me living is not "mine," but it is lived by faith of the Son of God, who loved me and gave himself for me. I am not going to go back on that.* (Galatians 2:19-21 MSG).

But the choice will be ours.

For many years we have received a gospel of what I call 'cross-less' Christianity. *"Come to Jesus and get blessed and your needs met".* No change, is required of you. You can stay exactly as you are and receive all the benefits.

To a certain extent that is true; salvation is by grace alone, not works, but we do not stop at salvation. That is simply the first step on our journey into maturity.

When we come to look at inheritance, we are looking at a completely different scenario; where changes *will* be required in order to qualify for the fulness of what is on offer.

God is bringing many *sons* to glory, not babes, fully mature sons. This is 'grown-up' stuff; meat, not milk.

We looked at the two lists, didn't we?

Paul says of them *'those who (continue to) do these things cannot inherit the Kingdom…'* 1 Corinthians 6: 9 – 10.

In these days Father is requiring us to come back to His word and begin to live our lives in alignment with it. That will mean we cannot continue to live our lives bent out of shape. We will have to straighten up.

The way that happens is that change needs to take place and change is here to stay. Smile please!

Prayer is perhaps a very simple example.

> *This is the confidence we have in approaching God: that if we ask anything according to his will, he hears us. And if we know that he hears us – whatever we ask – we know that we have what we asked of him.* (1 John 5:14-15 NIV)

The key words here are *'according to His will'*. That means seeking Him to find out what He wants to do and then asking Him to do it.

What *He* wants to do, you need to remember, often will not be what *you* want in the matter, but what He wants.

It is called Lordship. This is why I got you to make Him Lord as well as Saviour earlier on. You really cannot have one without the other.

On that simple issue, how is it working out for you?

Do you get 100% answers to prayer because you always seek Him on how to pray in any given situation; or would your view be that He does not answer prayer; or somewhere in between?

You can beat the dust out of the carpet until you are blue, beloved of God, but if you are not asking according to the Maker's desires, you will see no answers.

Sobering thought, but necessary at this point I think.

I will leave you with it.

19

Forgiveness

Something else that we brush under the carpet is the whole issue of forgiveness. But when we say the Lord's Prayer we are asking that He forgive us as we forgive others.

This message could be very short. How is it working out for you?

Seriously though, unforgiveness is an issue that can seriously affect your health, your inheritance and your peace, in the here and now.

You will not live in peace and harmony with anyone whilst you have bitterness and unforgiveness in your heart.

Sometimes we think we will take a look back over the past three days, but He is saying *let's go back thirty years'*.

Remember, He wants you to be free and un-forgiveness is solitary confinement. It locks you into a prison of your own making.

It also affects your physical and mental wellbeing, which is part of your inheritance. Do you see now how attitudes and behaviours are tied up with inheritance?

You can get pretty sick when you have un-forgiveness and bitterness at work in your life.

So how about it? Ask Him if there is anyone you need to forgive and be prepared to go back as far as He wants.

20

Institutionalised

Institutionalised. That is what we get when we *refuse* to come out of prison. We get used to living in bondage.

In fact, we are quite comfortable with it. Change presents us with a risk we are not prepared to take, even if that change is for the better.

But the cost of staying where we are far outweighs the benefits, if you would risk the north wind of change.

The definition of a rut is an open-ended grave. Are you stuck in a rut right now?

God, you know, resists us when we refuse to hear or see what He is saying to us over a lengthy period.

This does not happen overnight but little by little, as we refuse to hear the voice of whoever is sent to us to bring a mid-course correction. For whatever reason we are not going to listen to them and we determine not to hear. The result of this consistent hardening of our hearts can be spiritual deafness and/or blindness and sometimes even physical ailments.

It is not easy to say this without being perceived as judgmental; this is not my intention. It is for illustrative purposes only.

Whole denominations throughout church history have been awakened spiritually and have known the ability to hear the Lord's voice, but eventually they resisted Jesus when He sought to bring them a further revelation of Himself, and the entire denomination lost its way *and* its ability to hear what the Spirit was saying to the church in their day.

"I have this against you…" (Revelation 2 & 3).

The admonitions and counsel to the churches in the book of Revelation are very relevant, if we have ears to hear. If this were not so, He would not have had to write to them to call them back. It was ever thus:

"Let My people go that they might worship Me" (Exodus 8:1 NIV)

Moses' message to Pharaoh. He *always* calls us back to Himself. Not to gift, ministry, healing or deliverance, but to Himself.

I recall asking you before what particular Pharaoh had your attention?

It is perfectly possible to come to the place where you now want to understand the deeper things of the Spirit, but cannot. What is true for denominations is true for individuals also.

I emphasise this does not happen overnight, but little by little, over many, many years. Personally, I have observed it take place over more than twenty-five years. A persistent refusal to hear – and when I use the term 'hear' I mean hear with a view to changing your opinion; what you think; your mindset and your speed of obedience – results in both physical and spiritual deafness.

Not a good place to be. He is not unjust. You cannot plead that you didn't understand. He will have given you many, many opportunities to repent, change your mind and move your feet.

I did not read this in a book my darlings. I have seen it happen and it is tragic.

Has this hit your spot?

If it has, get with Him quickly and sort it out. Remember, not three days, more like 30 years!

God bless you.

21

Church versus Kingdom

I have said it before, doubtless I will say it again. Church and Kingdom are not the same thing.

Overemphasis on church, side-lines both the King and the Kingdom. But the Bible clearly says that one *governs* the other.

The Kingdom is governmental. It tells us how to run our lives. It instructs. It commands. We do not like that, rebels that we are!

Church grows out of Kingdom. Jesus did not come preaching the Gospel of the church. He came preaching the Gospel of the Kingdom; the Kingdom of God. The evidence of His Lordship in the lives of His people.

The Kingdom is constant and unchanging. The Kingdom is powerful and received by faith, as is its King.

The church is fluid, flexible, and should always be being upgraded. The church is not and cannot be a constant, but the Kingdom can and is; the Kingdom is immutable, it never, ever changes, like its King.

"Thy Kingdom come, Thy will be done…"

As we grow up in Jesus, the church we attend needs to change to reflect who we are becoming in the Kingdom, as we align ourselves with the rules of the Kingdom, as expressed by Jesus in His Sermon on the Mount.

Rules. Don't like those.

Government of God. Like that even less.

Let me bring you some inconvenient enlightenment at this point. There is no true freedom without rules or boundaries. The fallen human condition requires boundaries and rules. Human nature has a great deal of ungoverned desires rattling about.

For a start, it lacks self-control. When many talk about freedom we are actually saying, *'let me alone, I want to run my own life…'*

When the government of God comes it displaces everything else and causes inconvenience – big time. It is called light. It is called change.

And it is here to stay.

22

The emphasis is on obedience

Rules. Ah! Don't like those. Thought we were supposed to be free.

And obedience. Don't like that either – unless it is what I want to do, then it is different!

"If you love Me, you will …… Me" Kindly fill in the blank.

The Kingdom has rules. That may come as a shock, but there it is. Grace is not a licence to kill, despite what James Bond says.

Obedience in this regard means to hear with a view to doing what we are being asked to do.

> *"Not everyone who says to Me, 'Lord, Lord,' will enter the kingdom of heaven, but only he who does the will of My Father who is in heaven."* (Matthew 7:21 AMP).

Entrance into the Kingdom is what is at stake here, not salvation. And Jesus points now to the will of the Father. The Gospel is free but it is not cheap.

Aslan is good, but He isn't safe! *"Who said anything about safe? 'Course he isn't safe. But he's good. he's the King I tell you..."* says Mr. Beaver.[1]

> *"Why are you calling Me Lord, when you aren't doing what I am asking of you?"* Luke 6:46

Jesus wants us to *desire* to do the Father's will in just the same way as He desired to do the will of the Father.

We have said it before; the cross is where my will and God's will, cross. It is where our resentment, rebellion, recalcitrance, stubbornness and self-centeredness really show themselves.

Our desire to run the show according to our rules.

In an age where it is often said there are no absolute truths, we as His people must get back to finding out what His will for us really, really is and when we do, obeying it – in other words, following His rules.

For instance, when He says *'you shall not commit adultery'* (Exodus 20:14) we can think it is wrong because it breaks the marriage covenant and the trust between the parties concerned. This is not the primary concern here, it is wrong because *God says* it is wrong. And His is the highest authority.

Have we settled for something less do you think, and do we love to have it so?

Just a question you might like to answer in your own time. Why are you calling Me Lord?

The Ten Commandments are distinctly old fashioned so far as modern man is concerned, but what about God's view?

Did He really say? Are we being duped just like Adam and Eve in the garden, by questioning God's right to impose conditions on keeping that which He not only owns, but created, and loves and guards with a passion.

The earth is the Lord's and everything in it. Psalm 24:1.

Back to the drawing board maybe.

Note
1. The Chronicles of Narnia: 'The Lion the Witch and the Wardrobe' p 75 Diamond Books 1998.

23

The Church and the World

The person who wrote this poem in 1936, obviously thought that you could lose your salvation as is evidenced by the very last verse. But the content is so applicable to today and what I want to talk about next – which are addictions and adultery – that it seems good at this point to include it. It has no copyright:

The Church and the World:

"The Church and the World walked far apart
On the changing shores of time,
The World was singing a giddy song,
And the Church a hymn sublime.

"Come, give me your hand," said the merry World,
"And walk with me this way!"
But the faithful Church hid her gentle hands
And solemnly answered "Nay!

I will not give you my hand at all,
And I will not walk with you;
Your way is the way that leads to death;

Thy Kingdom Come

Your words are all untrue."

"Nay, walk with me but a little space,"
Said the World with a kindly air;
"The road I walk is a pleasant road,
And the sun shines always there.

Your path is thorny and rough and rude,
But mine is broad and plain;
My way is paved with flowers and dews,
And yours with tears and pain.

The sky to me is always blue,
No want, no toil I know;
The sky above you is always dark,
Your lot is a lot of woe.
There's room enough for you and me
To travel side by side."

Half shyly the Church approached the World
And gave him her hand of snow;
And the old World grasped it and walked along,
Saying, in accents low:

"Your dress is too simple to please my taste;
I will give you pearls to wear,
Rich velvets and silks for your graceful form,
And diamonds to deck your hair."

The Church looked down at her plain white robes,
And then at the dazzling World,
And blushed as she saw his handsome lip

Beryl Moore

With a smile contemptuous curled.

"I will change my dress for a costlier one,"
Said the Church, with a smile of grace;
And her pure white garments drifted away,
And the World gave, in their place,
Beautiful satins and shining silks,
Roses and gems and costly pearls;
While over her forehead her bright hair fell
Crisped in a thousand curls.

"Your house is too plain," said the proud old World,
"I'll build you one like mine;
With walls of marble and towers of gold,
And furniture ever so fine."

So he built her a costly and beautiful house;
Most splendid it was to behold;
Her sons and her beautiful daughters dwelt there
Gleaming in purple and gold.

Rich fairs and shows in the halls were held,
And the World and his children were there.
Laughter and music and feasts were heard
In the place that was meant for prayer.

There were cushioned seats for the rich and the gay,
To sit in their pomp and pride;
But the poor who were clad in shabby array,
Sat meekly down outside.

"You give too much to the poor," said the World.

Thy Kingdom Come

"Far more than you ought to do;
If they are in need of shelter and food,
Why need it trouble you?

Go, take your money and buy rich robes,
Buy horses and carriages fine;
Buy pearls and jewels and dainty food,
Buy the rarest and costliest wine.

My children, they dote on all these things,
And if you their love would win
You must do as they do, and walk in the ways
That they are walking in."

So the poor were turned from her door in scorn,
And she heard not the orphan's cry;
But she drew her beautiful robes aside,
As the widows went weeping by.

Then the sons of the World and the Sons of the Church
Walked closely hand and heart,
And only the Master, who knoweth all,
Could tell the two apart.

Then the Church sat down at her ease, and said,
"I am rich and my goods increase;
I have need of nothing, or aught to do,
But to laugh, and dance, and feast."
The sly World heard, and he laughed in his sleeve,
And mockingly said, aside:
"The Church is fallen, the beautiful Church;
And her shame is her boast and her pride."

Beryl Moore

The angel drew near to the mercy seat,
And whispered in sighs her name;
Then the loud anthems of rapture were hushed,
And heads were covered with shame.

And a voice was heard at last by the Church
From Him who sat on the throne:

"I know thy works, and how thou hast said,
'I am rich, and hast not known
That thou art naked, poor and blind,
And wretched before my face;'
Therefore from my presence cast I thee out,
And blot thy name from its place." [1]

It describes the world in the church, and specifically the one at Laodicea, the luke-warm church that was neither hot nor cold.

I wonder what you are this morning – hot or cold?

God forbid that you be found to be lukewarm.

Note
1. Matilda C. Edwards, Best Loved Poems (Garden City, NY: Garden City Publishing, 1936) pages 345-347.

24

Addiction and Adultery

We talked about adultery so we might as well include another 'A' word – Addiction…

As a race we are *addicted* to having our own way. Probably one of Frank Sinatra's best-known songs was *'I did it my way'*.

I used to like that one forty years ago; I identified with it of course, in those days. We are lovers and protectors of ourselves, aren't we?

You raise your eyebrows but examine your life for a moment; is it not full of I, me and mine a lot of the time? What I want, where I am going, my life plan, my will, and how I am going to achieve it; protect it and control the outcome; get what I want no matter what.

We are addicted to our will being done and if God should look as though He has another plan He wants us to follow, war breaks out.

That other word then: adultery. We have to join them together, addiction and adultery, because one leads to the other.

And Father has an interesting spin on it.

I counselled an alcoholic in the past that had a soul tie with alcohol. He literally loved it and though he was healed, he deliberately returned to drinking heavily. He subsequently died. Father said he was committing adultery.

There is a way that seems right to a man but the end thereof is death (Proverbs 14:12).

I know of someone else who was instantly delivered from smoking, but again, deliberately went straight back.

Perverse we are. We will have it our way, even if it kills us and sometimes it does.

Addiction and adultery go together.

Any uncontrolled desires, fuelled by the need to rule our own lives, find satisfaction in our own way, can have a disastrous effect on us because it leads to *spiritual* adultery; we walk away from God and His loving supervision of our lives – like the church at Ephesus – we leave first love.

Beloved we *need* rules. We need boundaries. We do not like them, but we desperately need them.

Addiction to our own will, plus uncontrolled desires, lusts and wrong motives cause fights and quarrels. They are the cause of wars.

Jesus' brother James had something to say about them

and it may surprise you:

Submit yourselves to God

What causes fights and quarrels among you? Don't they come from your desires that battle within you? You desire but do not have, so you kill. You covet but you cannot get what you want, so you quarrel and fight. You do not have because you do not ask God. When you ask, you do not receive, because you ask with wrong motives, that you may spend what you get on your pleasures.

You adulterous people, don't you know that friendship with the world means enmity against God? Therefore, anyone who chooses to be a friend of the world becomes an enemy of God. (James 4:1-4 NIV).

Adulterous people, he says not holding his punches. Friendship with the world, the way it thinks and what it seeks after, automatically puts you on the wrong side of God. Even makes you an enemy. Now there's a thought.

As your Lover and coming Husband, He sees it as adultery. Why? Because you are His bride, and if you are flirting with the world you are in danger of committing adultery – in a spiritual sense.

If you refuse to change your culture and remain in the ways of the world, you are reneging on your marriage agreement to cleave only to Him. You are breathing life into a corpse and there is the stench of death about you.

You are His bride. He is jealous over you.

Be sure He will come to get you and bring you to Himself. He is the ultimate Lover. Jealous for you.

You had never thought about that before? Maybe then it is time to sit down and think a bit more about these things?

The friends of the Bridegroom are placed on the earth to help the bride prepare for her Groom and coming King. They have a responsibility to see she does not continue to commit adultery with the world. They bring to her a mid-course correction; to create a change of direction.

Hello… thought I had lost you there for a moment.

His Majesty

The first requirement to enter this Kingdom then is to acknowledge that the King is supreme and His commands are to be obeyed; they are not to be seen as a burden.

He is your Lord and you are His love slave:

> *'The most important commandment is this: "Hear, O Israel, the Eternal One is our God, and the Eternal One is the only God. You should love the Eternal, your God, with all your heart, with all your soul, with all your mind, and with all your strength."* (Mark 12:28-30 The Voice)

The second – obedience:

> *And now, Israel, what is the Eternal your God asking of you? Only that you fear Him, live as He wants you to, and love Him; serve Him with every part of you, heart and soul;* (Deuteronomy 10:12-13 The Voice).

The third – *after* you have done the first two and not before – comes love your neighbour as you love yourself:

Jesus (quoting Scripture): "Love the Eternal One your God with all your heart and all your soul and all your mind. This is the first and greatest commandment. And the second is nearly as important, Love your neighbour as yourself. The rest of the law, and all the teachings of the prophets, are but variations on these themes."
(Matthew 22:37-40 The Voice)

Sorted.

Jesus made it clear He did not come to abolish any of the law or the commandments, but to fulfil them.

He fulfilled it perfectly because the law has to do with the inside of us, not the outside. He showed forth the character and nature of the Father by what He did and how He lived. When the inside is right, the outside will follow.

Culture affects conduct, and conduct follows character. After these, come influence. But we have a way to go before we talk about the fact that we are meant to be life changers and influence the atmosphere, the world where we are. We cannot do that if we are the same as them. There is no such thing as cultural relevance folks.

Now we have the King inside us, and He has brought His *culture* with Him, we have to bring ourselves into alignment with how He thinks and behaves. We are to bring His culture to bear on the world in which we live; we are to bring heaven to earth.

"Thy Kingdom come, Thy will be done..."

First in me. He gives us clear and detailed instructions on how to do this in Matthew 5-7.

We are about ready to begin now I think. What we have seen has been warm up to bring us to this place where we desire to do His will more than anything else.

That is where you are isn't it?

I will leave you to think that over and then we will really get stuck into this Kingdom living business.

26

Alignment

It is imperative that we come into alignment with Father in the way He thinks and perceives things; that we submit His will. To do this will require us to live the life He has given us in His Son; the new value system and mindsets. We need to stop our visits to the cemetery to talk to the corpse.

When God puts a rule in our path, we have a choice – old nature or new. Am I going to do this from the old seed or the new?

We can rebel *'I won't'*; we can resent *'I will but I don't like it'*; we can take independent action *'I'll do it my way thank you'*. Or we can submit and begin to live in the newness of life He has given us.

Choices.

One thing you can be absolutely sure about – God doesn't speak to your old man, that black dog, even if you persist in living there. It could go very, very quiet until you learn to move your feet and live life from the new place; the higher place.

At this point you do need to know that God does not change His mind or His rules for anyone. If you refuse to change the first time around, He will be back, again and again and again until you comply.

And you will make no forward movement until you do. You are really shooting yourself in the foot if you refuse to move.

Key here: God does not measure time, He measures growth. He is agricultural and in no hurry. You may think you have jumped that hurdle when the Coach says *"round it one more time please..."*

"Who does He think He is anyway, this is my life."

Difficult situations, circumstances and people have a habit of recurring in our lives until we see what Father is aiming at; alignment. Every time we go around it again, it gathers interest, compound interest, and it gets more difficult.

That is really worth remembering. Compound interest; it accrues, adds up, increases.

We all know by now that the mind set on the things of the flesh is at enmity, at war, with God; it resists Him.

> *For those who live according to the flesh set their minds on the things of the flesh, but those who live according to the Spirit, the things of the Spirit.* (Romans 8:5).

So what needs to happen is that we have a complete mindset

change. *"I was like this, now I am like that"* and then live our lives from there.

A change from being set on the things of the flesh; this world and what it seeks after for satisfaction, to where we are living from new; being set on the culture of heaven and what Father is looking at and for. Becoming Father pleasers, not man pleasers.

When your will is brought into alignment with the will of God, the *Kingdom of God* comes in your life.

The journey is called process. *"It doesn't happen all at once"* as the skin horse says, *"you become, it takes a long time."* [1]

And the first thing that needs to happen is that your focus must change, because what you behold you will become. If you are beholding the things of this life you will become very short-sighted indeed.

You need a new lens. Wide angle. Panoramic. Not myopic.

A new perspective. A new mindset. A new heart. A new understanding. And He has given you all these things in His Son. Yahoo!

Your job, with the Holy Spirit, is to make the choices that will bring you into alignment with His will rather than yours.

Not rocket science. But it can be painful, if you resist.

Now your choices will empower or disempower you. Each

choice will either make you more pliable and mouldable in His hands, or more like a piece of granite, unyielding and hard, brittle and sharp. We looked at people like that before, and we all know when we have bumped up against one of those.

Attitudes determine altitude. Choices have to do with destiny. You are predestined to be conformed to the image of Christ.

That is what this is all about. Your predestination. The midcourse corrections you need to make to ensure you reach your destination that has been chosen by your Father, because He knows what is best for you; you do not.

Note
1. 'The Original Velveteen Rabbit' Margery Williams, p 10 Egmont UK Ltd. 2004

27

Another look at values

We need to take another look at our values. It is so easy to slip back into seeking that which the world seeks after. Nothing wrong with that you may think, except that it has a negative effect on our forward movement.

Consider this: The world's system of privacy, material success, convenience and comfort. This produces: competition, striving, unfulfilled desires, stress, control, worry, frustration – fill in your own blank spaces.

You will, as the song says, *'get no satisfaction'*[1] if you live your life for yourself.

On the other hand, if you live your life for Him, you will find godliness and contentment with what you have is indeed great gain.

Let us just revisit Kingdom values again:

Openness and authenticity, sacrifice, love and discomfort. Amazingly these produce peace, rest, harmony, fulfilment, and contentment.

Contentment, now there's a word. Are you content with what you have this day?

Advertisements you know are designed to cause you to be discontent; to inflame your desire to possess something you do not have. They make you want something you perhaps never thought about before you saw the advert. Then it becomes a *'must have'*.

I walked into a shopping mall some years ago and heard *'buy, buy, buy'*. The whole world lies in the the wicked one.

Contentment is great gain, if it has godliness attached to it. The culture of the Kingdom. Completely 'other than' the culture of this world. I know which I would rather have.

The reason we need to revisit these things from time to time is that we forget. In the garden Eve told God that *'The serpent caused me to forget.'* (Genesis 3:13 Literal translation) Eve *forgot* who she was and what she was there for; Who created her and His eternal purpose for her.

Right there, with Jesus regularly spending time with them both, the serpent managed to allure Eve with the things of the world; the lust of the eye, the lust of the flesh and the pride of life. Immediately she desired that which was forbidden. She forgot she was created for love; for a love relationship with her Creator; for fellowship with Jesus.

Ever left a meeting thinking what an excellent word you had just heard and then found you could not remember a thing?

The serpent just caused you to forget. He does not change his ways.

There is a need to keep reminding ourselves where we are headed. Our destiny and our destination, planned by God from before the foundation of the world.

Like our little sailing vessel, when we tack we lose sight of where we are headed and have to bring ourselves back to remembrance of our identity, our destination and our destiny.

We will do that next.

Note
1. 'Satisfaction' Rolling Stones, 1965.

28

All this is His idea

*And we know that in all things God works for the good of those who love him, who have been called according to **his purpose**.* (Romans 8:28 NIV emphasis added).

'His purpose'

The Lord foils the plans of the nations; he thwarts the purposes of the peoples." But the plans of the Lord stand firm for ever, the purposes of his heart through all generations. (Psalm 33:10-11 NIV).

Stops you in your tracks doesn't it?

He did it. *Purposed* it. Everything, is because *He* purposed it. He is the architect; the author and the finisher of our faith.

Everything begins with Him and ends with Him and we are somewhere in the middle. God purposed, according to *His* will; everything.

"Thy Kingdom come."

He is working to a fixed point that we know nothing about. He is steering this little barque we call the church, and our individual lives, into His eternal purpose.

That is another thing well worth keeping in mind at this point; He plans for eternity. Everything He does and purposes has eternity in mind. Purpose and eternity.

No wonder we have to keep Majesty right in the forefront of our thinking. It is so easy to forget that all this not about me, but *Him.*

HIS MAJESTY

It is about eternity, not a short span on this earth. About His plan not mine.

When I get caught up in my little day-to-day problems and trivia, I need to take stock; take a broader view. Remember that far above the circle of the earth sits One so Majestic He is indescribable in His beauty and power. I need to:

> *Worship the Lord in the beauty of holiness, bow down before Him, His glory proclaim, gold of obedience and incense of lowliness, these are the offerings to bring to His Throne...*[1]

> *He has told you O man what is good, and what does the Lord require of you... but to act justly, love mercy and walk humbly with your God.* (Micah 6:8).

I remember. Isaiah says it like this:

Thy Kingdom Come

"To whom then will you liken Me,
Or to whom shall I be equal?" says the Holy One.
Lift up your eyes on high,
And see who has created these things,
Who brings out their host by number;
He calls them all by name,
By the greatness of His might
And the strength of His power;
Not one is missing.
"To whom will you liken Me?"
(Isaiah 40:25-26)

Gulp. 'No-one, Sir.'

"Listen to Me, O house of Jacob,
And all the remnant of the house of Israel,
Who have been upheld by Me from birth,
Who have been carried from the womb:
Even to your old age, I am He,
And even to grey hairs I will carry you!
I have made, and I will bear;
Even I will carry, and will deliver you.
"To whom will you liken Me, and make Me equal
And compare Me, that we should be alike?
Remember the former things of old,
For I am God, and there is no other;
I am God, and there is none like Me,
Declaring the end from the beginning,
And from ancient times things that are not yet done,
Saying, 'My counsel shall stand,
And I will do all My pleasure,'

...

Indeed I have spoken it;
I will also bring it to pass.
I have purposed it; I will also do it."
(Isaiah 46:1-5; 9-11).

I rest my case in reverence and awe.

Note
1. J S B Monsell, Baptist Hymnal, number 35.

29

This instant age

This is the age of instant everything. Add hot water and stir; everything from porridge and soup to wallpaper paste – for which, incidentally, you need cold water.

Internet connection, immediate access 24/7 to everything and anything; order and get same day delivery. We know nothing of delayed gratification; we cannot wait.

And it is all over the Christian scene. Information overload and cannot wait. *'Transform your prayer life in 4 minutes a day.' 'The one-minute bible...'*[1]

Never let it be said that we have to linger more than ten seconds on anything. Instant gratification. Everything must be instantly recognisable and satisfy the urgent need of the moment or it is no good.

Whatever happened to: *those who wait on the Lord...* (Isaiah 40:31 KJV)

Wait. Sit, stay, remain, wait.

Someone advised me when I went into video production *'You have to grab their attention in ten seconds or you'll lose them.'* What an indictment.

Yet I find one of the things Father wants me to teach is stillness. Contemplation. Waiting. Followed by silence and solitude.

Simplicity. Submission and finally Surrender.

He has not changed *His* way of doing things. He requires us to come before Him in exactly the same way as He always did.

"Sanctify yourselves, for tomorrow..." (Joshua 3:5).

Joshua gives the order for all the people who are to cross the Jordan into their Promised Land in the morning, to sanctify themselves, to get themselves ready, to abstain from certain things and to do others.

What does that mean sanctify yourselves? Separate yourselves to Him alone, do what He says.

He is the Creator, you are the created. He is God. You are not. He never changes.

Shoreless ocean who can sound Thee,
Thine own eternity is round Thee
Majesty sublime.[2]

Sanctify yourselves. Set yourselves apart. Make sure you are clean, because tomorrow we are on the move and there are giants in the land and battles to be fought and won; we need some changes and some discipline here.

Notes

1. Titles observed in a Christian bookshop.
2. The Christian book of Mystical Verse, p 7, A W Tozer, Christian Publications, 1963.

30

Badger skins

I can, and do, get on some people's nerves. Often. A lot.
I see things from His perspective, not theirs. That bugs
them.

Because I love Him. Alone. First and foremost. Because I
love Him, I cannot stop talking about Him.

I think we should defer to Him in all things, not just some
things. I pray about everything. Defer to Him. That bugs
some people too.

Sets me apart as different. Not normal. Too single-minded.
Too intense...

Lighten up! Live a little! I am.

In the Presence. In the glory. I just happen to be wearing
a badger skin. Remember that? The tabernacle in the
wilderness was covered with them so they hid the glory.

We are like that. We have this treasure in earthen vessels.
The treasure we contain is Jesus; the Kingdom is within us.

Thy Kingdom Come

The earthen vessel our body; is the badger skin. The glory is only visible to those who know Him.

The only place to be is where He is. In the Most Holy Place. Before the Mercy seat, the Throne of Grace. Touching heaven, touching earth.

No earthly use otherwise. A heavenly mindset is needed.

His Kingdom coming into us. The culture of heaven coming to earth. His will coming down, through me.

How about you? Are you hovering somewhere between heaven and earth?

Are you an earthbound eagle or are you living in heavenly places, in Christ?

You choose and go on choosing.

31

We are captive to our culture

They say if you put a frog in cold water and heat it up it won't jump out. It is called gradualism; putting it in cold water and it does not notice it is being killed. Death creeps up on it gradually and by the time the frog realises it is too late to jump out.

It is what we as a *'nation within a nation'* are suffering from. Gradualism. We are captive to our culture.

It has been so insidious we have not noticed the change in our vocabulary as children of God, and citizens of the Kingdom. We have gone from being a *'holiness'* people and a people who are *'consecrated'* to Him (set apart for Him) to something so ignoble as to be irreconcilable with what the Bible holds out as our standard for living.

"Be holy for I am I am holy." (1 Peter 1:16 NKJV)

We started somewhere like that, with something about being perfect as our heavenly Father is perfect.

A Future in God

So roll up your sleeves, put your mind in gear, be totally ready to receive the gift that's coming when Jesus arrives. Don't lazily slip back into those old grooves of evil, doing just what you feel like doing. You didn't know any better then; you do now. As obedient children, let yourselves be pulled into a way of life shaped by God's life, a life energetic and blazing with holiness. God said, "I am holy; you be holy." (1 Peter 1:13-16 MSG).

What has happened to us is called declension. A deterioration, a decline, a downward slide. We have become captive to our culture.

But all is not lost. There is a way back. He never gives up on us.

Place Your Life Before God

So here's what I want you to do, God helping you: Take your everyday, ordinary life – your sleeping, eating, going-to-work, and walking-around life – and place it before God as an offering. Embracing what God does for you is the best thing you can do for him. Don't become so well-adjusted to your culture that you fit into it without even thinking. Instead, fix your attention on God. You'll be changed from the inside out. Readily recognise what he wants from you, and quickly respond to it. Unlike the culture around you, always dragging you down to its level of immaturity, God brings the best out of you, develops well-formed maturity in you. (Romans 12:1 MSG).

Today is the day of salvation. We are saved, we are being saved, and we will be saved. From ourselves and our culture.

He will have a people for Himself. He is coming for His own.

But we do have a choice. That word again. It is what life in the Spirit is all about. Choices. Continual choices. Not just once, but all day every day.

Until perfected at last we stand before Him, *'clothed in His righteousness alone, faultless to stand before the Throne.'*[1]

I will have some of that, how about you?

Note
1. 'My Hope is Built on Nothing Less', Edward Mote, c 1834

SECTION 3

Life from a higher place

Love God and live as you please. For the soul trained in love to God will do nothing to offend the One who is beloved.

Augustine[1]

1

Without Me, you can do nothing

Now when Jesus saw the crowds, he went up on a mountainside and sat down. His disciples came to him, and he began to teach them. He said:

"Blessed are the poor in spirit, for theirs is the kingdom of heaven.
Blessed are those who mourn, for they will be comforted.
Blessed are the meek, for they will inherit the earth.
Blessed are those who hunger and thirst for righteousness, for they will be filled.
Blessed are the merciful, for they will be shown mercy.
Blessed are the pure in heart, for they will see God.
Blessed are the peacemakers, for they will be called children of God.
Blessed are those who are persecuted because of righteousness, for theirs is the kingdom of heaven."
(Matthew 5:1-10 NIV).

There are crowds here, a mixture of disciples, believers, and followers, all waiting open mouthed for what He is about to say.

But it is to the *disciples*, the continuers, that He speaks as they come to Him.

Many in that crowd we know, will walk or drift away, when the importance of His words sinks in. It is therefore to the *disciples* that He speaks, His apprentices, learners, continuers, those closest to Him. The inner circle.

His words have a way of separating the hearers. Initially they are received with joy, but when the cares of the world and the deceitfulness of riches come, the hearers drop away.

It is those who will endure the consequences of the words who continue. *'You are those who have continued with Me in my trials…'*

If you want to follow Me, continue with Me, walk in My way; there is only one path and these are the conditions.

Count yourselves blessed when you are poor in spirit, when you mourn your spiritual poverty, when you hunger and thirst for righteousness.

When you:

> Forsake all that you have.
> Rely totally on Me.
> Go wherever I send.
> Do whatever I ask.
> Suffer whatever I allow.

At the centre of the universe is a cross. *"On that day many will call Me Lord."* (Matthew 7:22).

Stark choices; stark contrast to anything they have ever heard from the teachers of the law.

Yet they are drawn, inexplicably, to desire this life; this communion; this communication; this deep relationship with Him.

They *do* hunger and thirst for the righteousness of which He speaks. For the ability to love without ceasing; to allow their worldly goods to be destroyed and stolen without retaliating or seeking recompense. But they know of a certainty that in their natural strength, they cannot do any of it, any more than they could keep the law.

This life can only be lived in the power of the Holy Spirit and no other way.

"Blessed are the meek, for they will inherit the earth."

Meek is to be humbly patient or docile under the provocation of others. All this is totally impossible.

This does not describe the life of the natural man, but of the man who is filled with the Spirit of God, the Enabler; the One who will work into us the righteous life of which Jesus speaks.

In the Sermon on the Mount Jesus introduces the One whom He will ask the Father to send when He has completed His task of redemption.

The Holy Spirit, for without *Him*, we can do nothing.

Absolutely nothing.

Note
1. www.wedgewords.wordpress.com

2

You are blessed

Before He deals with anything else, Jesus talks about the nature of the people who will inherit the earth and the Kingdom. He describes them as poor and mourning.

> *When Jesus saw his ministry drawing huge crowds, he climbed a hillside. Those who were apprenticed to him, the committed, climbed with him. Arriving at a quiet place, he sat down and taught his climbing companions. This is what he said: "You're blessed when you're at the end of your rope. With less of you there is more of God and his rule."* (Matthew 5:1-2 MSG).

Jesus tells His disciples that when they are really happy and totally fulfilled; when they are most blessed and qualify for entry into the Kingdom of God is when they are at the end of themselves. God starts when we reach the end of ourselves; our rope the Message calls it, and until we come to that place, He cannot begin.

There's a thought right there.

We are taught to be self-sufficient and it carries over into our Christian life, but Jesus says the very opposite.

When you have come to the absolute end of all your trying and striving, and sink exhausted, fully recognising your need, then and only then, can the *Kingdom* begin to come, *really* come, in your life. Only then, can His government begin to take effect.

In the Kingdom, as we have said before, the way up is down.

In a classic one liner Jesus says *'if you are feeling desperate about yourself, hopeless, helpless, useless, unworthy and totally empty – you are happy indeed!'*

Being poor in spirit has to do with self-evaluation. If you are religiously rich and okay in your own estimation, forget it. Because being *poor* in spirit is your qualification for Kingdom life. When you cannot do it, have not got a snowball's chance and you know it; that He says is an excellent place to be.

You cannot help someone who does not know that they have a problem.

The opening words then to this classic Sermon are that if you feel no sense of self-worth, walk right in, the answer is here and you are *so* blessed.

Conversely, the confident, self-sufficient and self-righteous, kindly take a seat, wait outside until He has dealt with your pride. You do not yet qualify for entry into the Kingdom.

Thy Kingdom Come

If you are poor in spirit and you know you have not even scratched the surface of the Christian walk, the Kingdom of heaven is yours.

But not otherwise.

3

Character, behaviour and influence

We will begin to see that the Sermon teaches us about three things:

Character;
Behaviour;
Influence.

As we recognise our spiritual poverty and change our minds about who we thought we were, and what we think we know, we mourn, which leads us to *repentance* – we turn around. In doing this our conduct and *behaviour* change, which in turn influences everything and everyone around us.

One of the first requirements is that we *mourn* – we are distressed over our own spiritual state and our poverty of spirit. We really do see with Paul that in us *'dwells no good thing'* apart from Jesus.

That gives us a good springboard for the next promise we bump into in the Sermon on the Mount:

"Blessed are those who mourn, for they will be comforted."

It's something to be happy about!
You will be blessed by the comfort of the Holy Spirit, who is the Comforter, as you mourn your spiritual state, repent and change your mind.

'Repentance', said Basilea Schlink, *'is a joy'*. She was so convinced about this she wrote a book on the subject *'Repentance, the joy-filled life'*[1], but she was not the first one. Hear king David when he was discovered in his sin with Bathsheba:

1. *"Look on me with a heart of mercy, O God, according to Your generous love. According to Your great compassion, wipe out every consequence of my shameful crimes.*
2. *Thoroughly wash me, inside and out, of all my crooked deeds. Cleanse me from my sins.*
3. *For I am fully aware of all I have done wrong, and my guilt is there, staring me in the face.*
4. *It was against You, only You, that I sinned, for I have done what You say is wrong, right before Your eyes. So when You speak, You are in the right. When You judge, Your judgments are pure and true.*
5. *For I was guilty from the day I was born, a sinner from the time my mother became pregnant with me."* (Psalm 51:1-5 NIV)

Look at verse 4: *It was against You, only You, that I sinned, for I have done what You say is wrong, right before Your eyes.*

David sees against whom He has actually committed this sin and it is not Uriah or Bathsheba, but against God Himself. You can find the story in 2 Samuel 11.

Someone else in the Bible had a sharp shock and realised they were not as righteous as they had imagined. This was their reaction:

The Damascus Road: Saul Converted

Then Saul, still breathing threats and murder against the disciples of the Lord, went to the high priest and asked letters from him to the synagogues of Damascus, so that if he found any who were of the Way, whether men or women, he might bring them bound to Jerusalem.

As he journeyed he came near Damascus, and suddenly a light shone around him from heaven. Then he fell to the ground, and heard a voice saying to him, "Saul, Saul, why are you persecuting Me?"

And he said, "Who are You, Lord?"

Then the Lord said, "I am Jesus, whom you are persecuting. It is hard for you to kick against the goads." So he, trembling and astonished, said, "Lord, what do You want me to do?" (Acts 9:1-6)

Saul, who becomes Paul, thinks he is doing the right thing killing Christians, but God says it is Him he is persecuting. It is the Lord he is resisting and to his credit, he swiftly changes his mind.

Taken right back to the source, God is the One against whom we sin, every single time and we find we need to repent.

Repentance results in a joy-filled heart; a heart, which is happy to unlearn what it thought it knew.

Pride has no place here. This heart acknowledges that it knows nothing and is willing to learn and go on learning; to change and go on changing. It is a heart willing to forget all it understood hitherto and turn its face into the wind of the Spirit.

Our heart is willing to hear and humbly admit it was wrong. It will make reparation and restoration where necessary. It takes the lower place, adopts the position of a child intent on learning.

It is characterised by submission, obedience, humility and meekness. After mourning and comfort, repentance produces a joy-filled life.

Note
1. 'Repentance, the joy-filled life' M. Basilea Schlink, Evangelical Sisterhood of Mary, Radlett, Hertfordshire, UK.

4

Blessed are the meek

"Blessed are the meek, for they will inherit the earth."
(Matthew 5:5 NIV)

Here we come with this inheritance business again. The promise to the meek, the submissive in heart, is that they will inherit something – the earth.

What would that look like?

Reigning and ruling; occupying that which is yours; it's called dominion and it was what Adam had and lost. Jesus, the Second Adam, won it back for us, but we have to press into what He has obtained in order to inherit.

No pain, no gain; no-one drifts to the top of a mountain; a backbone not wishbone, is needed here. Inheritance is a constant theme in the Kingdom.

As we have seen we can give it away like Adam; trade it like Esau; or disqualify ourselves by our behaviour.

Paul constantly warned that bad behaviour would *preclude*

entrance into the Kingdom and therefore gaining our inheritance; the reign and rule of the King in our lives. Take a look at 1 Corinthians 6 and Galatians 5 sometime, it is all in there.

The Kingdom is when the rule of the King is constant and continual in our lives. It requires discipline and discipline is not my claim on Jesus but the evidence of His claim on me. I do not 'make' Him Lord, I acknowledge His Lordship; His right to me as a blood bought believer, and my full intention to do His will however that may manifest itself.

If He cannot co-habit with the things mentioned in 1 Corinthians 6 and Galatians 5 I need to do something about it to get into alignment with Him.

Light and darkness cannot live together. If I care about my intimate relationship with Him, I will want to please Him and will do whatever is necessary to achieve that.

Once we accept Jesus as our King; once we come under the benevolent dictatorship of the Holy Spirit, our government is changed forever. We *begin* our Kingdom journey.

We allow the King to change our character into His:

From the distant past, His eternal love reached into the future. You see, He knew those who would be His one day, and He chose them beforehand to be conformed to the image of His Son so that Jesus would be the firstborn of a new family of believers, all brothers and sisters. As for those He chose beforehand, He called them to a

233

*different destiny so that they would experience what it
means to be made right with God and share in His glory.*
(Romans 8:29-30 The Voice)

We are being *conformed* to His image.

This has been God's plan from the foundation of the earth –
someone like Him in nature and character with whom He can
have fellowship.

He cannot fellowship with our fallen nature. He had to put
Adam and Eve out of the Garden when they fell.

When we come back into a love relationship with Him we
must be changed into His likeness and we need schooling on
how to live this new life.

We are destined to be conformed to His image.

The very first step is voluntarily to say 'yes' to this
transformation process because you cannot say 'No' and
'Lord' in the same sentence. Peter tells us in 2 Peter 1 that
these things are incremental.

We retain each virtue as we move on. They build on one
another, so we never forget our first lesson, but build our
character steadily and surely, by adding to our realisation of
our poverty and mourning for what we are not; a longing to
achieve a *higher place* from which to live.

We climb, staying broken and dignifying any trial that God, in
His wisdom, allows.

This Kingdom life is totally unlike anything we have ever seen before. It requires a marathon mentality.

Meekness is humility in action. You cannot be proud and meek at the same time. Meekness is self-effacing. It is the opposite of self-righteousness, arrogance and pride. It does not boast in its accomplishments. It is unpretentious, gentle and sweet in nature. It is not defensive and does not attack.

Meekness is an inner strength that accepts correction or criticism without sulking or needing to retaliate. It is humbly patient and docile under the provocation of others.

How is it working out for you?

5

When being hungry is a blessing

"Blessed are those who hunger and thirst for righteousness, for they will be filled."

Since when has being hungry and thirsty been a blessing? It is that upside down Kingdom again.

Now Jesus tells those who are continuing with Him – his apprentices, learners, disciples – that they are really blessed when they are hungry and thirsty for the righteousness that He speaks about.

Being in this state of desperation means that you are *very* focussed, because until you get filled you are not going to be satisfied! There is more than a degree of desperation here.

Are you desperate to live a righteous life? Do you really, really want, above all else to be righteous? Is it a hunger and thirst?

Perhaps we need to define just what righteousness looks like, then you can make an informed decision. Actually, it is easier to say what it is not than what it is. For a start it is not seeking justice, or vindication if you have been wronged.

What Jesus is talking about here is *internal*; the state of the heart.

Moral rectitude – lovely word "rectitude": decency, goodness, honesty, integrity, virtue, morality (there's old-fashioned), uprightness, and transparency; a heart, that if it is wronged does not seek retaliation or vindication, but turns the other cheek; a meek and humble heart.

This is all *internal*; the Holy Spirit produces it in our hearts as we co-operate with Him.

The righteousness of the Pharisees was seen – they made sure it was – it was outward. True righteousness is invisible and internal.

The righteousness Jesus spoke of seemed impossible to those who were listening because the Holy Spirit, the Enabler, had not yet been given.

In the natural it *is* impossible. But He never asks us to do or be something that He has not already given us.

That which was *imputed to us* at our rebirth – the legal transaction when we received His righteousness as a gift – is now being worked in, or *imparted*, by the indwelling Holy Spirit.

We have the goods. We are of all people most blessed!

Now, we develop an active dislike for the things which we previously craved, seemingly by no effort of our own. We begin to see what we lack spiritually and we mourn. It is at this point we develop a hunger and thirst for the righteousness that exceeds the Law, the written code.

This new way of life is so liberating it is addictive. James says it like this:

> *Therefore, get rid of all moral filth and the evil that is so prevalent, and humbly accept the word planted in you, which can save you.* (James 1:21 NIV)

Yes Sir!

Saved by grace alone by the *word* that has been planted in us.

What or Who is the word? John 1:14 and Revelation 19:13 reveals *Jesus* is the Word that has been planted in us. He became flesh and dwelt among us, remember?

Our part? Simply to co-operate with His indwelling Holy Spirit. To yield.

Which leads to a hunger and thirst for more. Brilliant.

Is this your experience?

Congratulations! All is grace. Christ is being formed in you.

6

What are you currently apologising to God for?

We talked about hungering and thirsting last time.

Character and behaviour, how we conduct ourselves, leading to the influence we exert where we are.

So, what are you apologising to God for? That is the result of the hunger and thirst. It is what God is doing *in* you to make you more like Himself.

His goal is to conform you to the image of His Son, in order that you might be a fit companion for Him throughout eternity.

As we become more God-conscious, rather than self-conscious, we find that we are apologising more frequently to God for our thoughts and behaviours.

"Here I go again, sorry Lord..." Ever done that? Character and conduct.

What is happening is that you are becoming increasingly

aware of the sinful nature that still seeks its own within you and you are developing a hunger and thirst not to be like that anymore.

You are daily putting that thing to death. We discover we cannot excuse our old nature by calling it *'only being human'*. We are taking responsibility for our own spiritual progress.

How the Spirit and the Word find us out. We are prone to say lamely, *'But everyone does it';* His response, *'Not you, we have another way, let Me show you'.*

No hiding place. What we are experiencing is the way these beautiful 'beatitudes' build on one another.

When God has shown us something, He loves to make it real in our experience. That is spelled P.A.I.N.F.U.L. because it is death on the instalment plan.

We discover we are blessed happy, joyful, as we become more aware of our spiritual poverty, and as the Holy Spirit begins to make real *in our experience* what His infilling means, we begin to mourn, as we see what darkness we have tolerated in our own hearts and lives; that leads us to start apologising to God for not being more like Christ in our thought life and behaviours; in our reactions to life's circumstances.

Gradually we become responders, rather than reactors. Thermostats, rather than thermometers. Steady, rather than tossed about.

Change is here to stay. Blessed, happy indeed are we if we

begin now to actually hunger and thirst for more Christlikeness in our lives, to desire it, actively to seek after it.

Not outward show, but inward transformation.

The seeking heart. The captivated heart. The heart's desire now to please Him above all else.

Walking with Him, aware of His indwelling, becoming ever increasingly sensitive to the nuances of the Holy Spirit and His voice...

How is it working out?

7

The quality of mercy

'The quality of mercy is not strained, it drops as the dew from heaven': the person who wrote that knew a thing or two... William Shakespeare the Merchant of Venice.

"Blessed are the merciful, for they will be shown mercy."

The seventh beatitude.

This says that you are blessed, happy, fulfilled and satisfied when you are merciful and that you in turn will receive mercy... hmmmm says something similar somewhere else I think...

"And forgive us our debts,
as we also have forgiven our debtors."
(Matthew 6:12 NIV)

'You don't know what they did...'

'Father forgive them' (Luke 23:34)

Mercy, something we all want to receive it but do not always pass on, in fact, if we are completely honest, we rarely pass it on. If we did there would be no strife, divisions, factions, arguments, un-forgiveness, bitterness, rivalry and splits within the church and the family.

So busy we are getting the speck out of someone else's eye, whilst we look straight past the log in our own.

Consider if you will, the parable of the unmerciful servant, forgiven a huge sum; debt wiped out completely, he goes free. Then he promptly goes out and beats the daylights out of his servant for a few pounds. (Matthew 24-30).

The man completely missed the point. He could not see his own sinfulness, and for the small misdemeanour of another, he berated, threatened and beat him. Terrible.

But aren't we like that? God has forgiven us so much but in our self-righteousness we really do not see it; we don't get it. We spend our time criticising and condemning others, unmindful of the fact that we are just proving our own need of mercy – yet again.

God you see is not looking at the other fellow, He is looking at you.

Wretched, poor and blind we are.

Having decided that we want to hunger and thirst after the righteousness imputed to us, we will be tested, and somehow or other you will find some really mean people coming your way which will give you the opportunity to act towards them in forgiveness and mercy, rather than revenge.

The word will begin to become flesh on you. Shredded flesh actually. Crucified flesh.

To follow the path of mercy will hurt. A lot. Satan offered Jesus a cross-less crown too, one that did not hurt.

Those people who have been the meanest to you will be the ones on the top of God's *'forgiveness list'* for you.

The bitterness, resentment and maybe even hatred that you have stored up in your heart towards them will be the first thing He wants to get rid of. Why? Because it is harming you and your relationship with Him, your ability to inherit the Kingdom. You will not be free until you release them from your un-forgiveness.

In order to be blessed, you are going to have to bite the bullet, forgive and release those prisoners you have held for so long…

Mercy. Beautiful word. Wonderful to receive it. Difficult to pass on in our old nature.

Which is where the choice comes in again old (human) nature or new (spiritual) nature? You get to choose.

But remember, you will not receive the mercy you need until you forgive and release the other fellow; it's the way it works. Consider this –

> *"For if you forgive other people when they sin against you, your heavenly Father will also forgive you. But if*

you do not forgive others their sins, your Father will not forgive your sins." (Matthew 6:14-15).

I will leave it with you.

Oh, before I do, would a pencil and paper help to write your list? I would not want you to leave anyone out; you would lose a blessing if you did!

8
Lingering here

I want to linger on this whole question of mercy for a moment, because to the extent that we show it, is the extent to which we will receive it. It indicates the extent to which we want God's Kingdom, His government, His rule and reign in our lives.

It is a good measurement for us. A rule of thumb to see where we are. If we are unwilling at this point, because of child-hood abuse, personal damage and hurt, to forgive and release those who wounded us, we are actually saying *"I can't go that far God".*

We are looking at the litmus test of our desire for Him and His Kingdom to come in our lives. You can have as much of Him as you want.

This could be self-limiting.

The question really is, how *do* you think and behave towards those who have hurt you deeply? Those who have offended you?

Do you make them feel guilty, or endeavour to punish them in some way? Maybe you just avoid them; do you withhold yourself from them, or are you gracious towards them?

Being merciful is showing grace from the heart when others have hurt you deeply, let you down and rejected you, amongst other things. It is setting aside the need for justice, as you see it, to be done.

It is not putting on a smile to conceal your feelings, or shunning them to show them how much they have hurt you. This is why showing mercy hurts. Personally and a lot.

You are choosing to let them off your hook. They did do that thing for years, but you are not going after them for your pound of flesh. You are acting in a *godly* way towards them.

You are certainly not dealing them the card they deserve. You are choosing to waive any claim you may justly have against them, just as your Father does towards you, and showing them mercy.

Mercy is not strained, it drops gently as the dew from heaven. Mercy triumphs over judgement. (James 2:13).

So how about it beloved? What is it going to be for you this day?

Are you going to kiss vindication goodbye and accept not only will they not get punished, but also you are happy that they will appear to be getting away with it?

Mercy. It is how He has dealt with you.

You are off the hook for all the bad things you have been thinking about them and the revenge you wanted, maybe even planned.

Remember you could be paying for your sins but you are not, by His mercy, He has paid the debt for you. Now He is saying to you *'You be that way too if you want to inherit my Kingdom'*.

You need to decide because the next thing we are going to look at is purity of heart, without which no-one will see the Lord.

9

Romance or reality

I feel the need to take a diversion here right now into what I would call romance or reality.

Part of my remit is to show you not so much the *romance*, but the *reality* of walking with Jesus. When His face is set as flint, we see a different Jesus.

We have to ask ourselves, do we still want to walk with Him where He is headed when He looks like this?

I began to think about how much we fall in love with the idea of being disciples; of going the whole way with Jesus. The romance, living in fulness not measure, and at the same time the thought came: *'starters'*.

The *'starters'* here referred to are those appetising little morsels we enjoy before the main course in a restaurant. Sometimes I enjoy them so much I would settle for a starter and a dessert and forget the main course; the meaty bit, the bit that takes some chewing and digesting.

Many of us fall into this category, we like the sound of

what Jesus is talking about and dash around the celestial supermarket filling our trolleys with good things. Then comes the check-out. Time to pay the Man.

He comes saying, *'I'll have this now please...'* That which we gave Him in a time of peace He is asking for now and we find we are in a time of war.

And like Abram before us, we find ourselves with the knife suspended over our particular Isaac – that is if we get that far.

Problem is, it is at that point most often we either abandon the trolley or rush to put everything we have collected back on the shelves.

I have seen it beloved, I have seen it, so many times. Enthusiasm in the heat and emotion of the moment, *"I want all You have Lord". "Count me in I am yours unreservedly". "Bring it on!"*

Then, in the cold light of day when He comes asking for what we voluntarily gave Him, we back off. Fast.

"No! Not that!! Ask me something else".

No condemnation. He does not do that. Just time to face *ourselves* squarely. We need to know our limits. What we really *will* commit to.

Horrible word that – commitment. But we have to face it.

What man building a tower does not sit down and count the

cost first? (Luke 14:28) What man going to war, ditto? What person joining Jesus's movement, does not sit down and look at what it is going to cost them in terms of time, family, money, commitment to His cause?

Movement means just that – we get to move. Are we in love with the idea? Or are we in love with Him?

It is going to be one or the other.

I will leave you to think that one through just now before we get back on track, because this Sermon on the Mount is going to do a work of separation in us.

First, hear Paul on the subject:

> Be Holy
> *"Come out from among them*
> *And be separate, says the Lord.*
> *Do not touch what is unclean,*
> *And I will receive you."*
> *"I will be a Father to you,*
> *And you shall be My sons and daughters,*
> *Says the Lord Almighty."*
> (2 Corinthians 6:11-18).

There will be some *'coming out'* before we are through with this thing.

10

Vain imaginings

I thought I had finished with the subject of counting the cost but the Lord had other ideas.

'Vain imaginings' He said.

'A crisis of faith' He said.

'Disillusionment' He said.

'I thought', He said.

Ah...I knew what He was talking about.

'Vain imaginings', these romantic thoughts about situations; day-dreams; playing situations out in your head and seeing them come to the conclusion you want.

Then they don't come to the conclusion you want. *'A crisis of faith'*; we get this when we expected Him to do something in a certain way; were convinced that we were *'in faith'* about it, and it all went pear-shaped.

The person died. Nothing happened. We didn't get that job; the money; the transfer, the big house, the ministry – fill in your own area.

We were devastated, we had *'a crisis of faith'* because we were disillusioned.

'Disillusioned'. Bottom line here is that you had an illusion in the first place. Something you dreamed up. Not something He had said and confirmed and continued to confirm. A dream.

'We thought', or I thought, as I did at the beginning of this little section. I thought I had quite finished, but He comes, *'not quite My darling...'*

The disciples on the road to Emmaus *'thought'* – and they thought wrong. They thought He was going to conquer the Romans; that they were going to be victorious and have their country back. They did not think He was going to die a criminal's death.

They were all of those I have mentioned. They imagined, they had a crisis. They were most of all disillusioned. Everything in ruins.

"I go fishing" Peter said. *"I'm going back to what I know. There is no point hanging around here, nothing's going to happen. It's all over, He's dead. (John 21 paraphrase).*

When we get caught up in our own day-dreaming He has to bring us to that crisis of faith. That place of disillusionment because we are not in reality, we are in romance.

We will all live happily ever after, but it is just not yet. Meanwhile, in the here and now, life is real, life is earnest.

We above all people must see things as they really, really are, not as we would like them to be.

He has to bring what Bob Mumford would call *'a dose of consummate reality'* into our lives. It came to him when he wanted to be a doctor and was attending his first operation. The surgeon opened the patient up and closed them up again. Inoperable. Bob received a dose of consummate reality. He was not going to be able to help some people, they were just too far-gone. In any event, God had another plan for his life.

If we are subject to day-dreaming or any of the other things I have mentioned, we need to be renewed in our minds.

We need to develop purity of heart, the next beatitude we will be looking at.

What's purity of heart? A heart without guile. It does not imagine things the way it wants them to be but trusts in Him and His word in all things. It does not day-dream. It is not subject to disillusionment. It is rooted and grounded in reality, in Christ and His resurrection life.

It is real and authentic. It is called faith and faith leaps. Fear on the other hand only looks.

How is it working out for you?

11

Pioneers or settlers: a captivated heart

Before we go on to look at what purity of heart means, we need to look at the captivated heart, so you can establish whether you are a pioneer or a settler.

A captivated heart is the difference between a pioneer and a settler.

A heart that has been *captivated* by Jesus will be both a disciple and a pioneer; they are in a race and they cannot stop.

'There's no stopping', Smith Wigglesworth is quoted as saying, *'in the Spirit filled life.*[1]

Settlers do just that. Settle. But settlers can only settle, to an extent, because they will find that life will never be the same again once they receive Jesus.

They can desire a life of peace but if they do, they have forgotten that God cannot spell and He spells peace with a 't' – tribulation, trouble.

Trouble, tribulation, works patience, peace and all those good things. In other words, character

> *We continue to shout our praise even when we're hemmed in with troubles, because we know how troubles can develop passionate patience in us, and how that patience in turn forges the tempered steel of virtue.* (Romans 5:3 MSG).

In the world you will have tribulation, Jesus said so.

Not Great Tribulation, that is different. Notice the capital letters.

This is about change. Regardless of whether you like it or not, whether you are a pioneer or a settler, change is here to stay.

God hasn't finished with you yet. You cannot cut across the park on this one.

Pioneers frequently find themselves in the position of being in a stuck place. Unable to go back because they know it will kill them; terrified to go forward because of what is in front of them. It is at this point they wish they had never embarked on the journey in the first place!

This is normal. Fear is normal. You *will* find yourself out of your depth, apprehensive and at times downright scared on this journey into the heart of God.

But He *always* brings you through. He *always 'leads you in triumphal procession.'*

Following Jesus, you are discovering, is not a Sunday school picnic. That is why we looked at the cost of being a disciple, a pioneer, before we went any further.

If you happen to have a captivated heart, of all people you are most blessed, because your heart has been captured, taken prisoner, by the King of Kings and Lord of Lords. You cannot do anything but be His love slave, fear and all.

Now that is sorted, we will take a look at what purity of heart looks like then.

Note
1. 'Smith Wigglesworth on Spirit filled living,' Whitaker House, source Googlebooks.co.uk.

12

Blessed are the pure in heart

"Blessed are the pure in heart, for they will see God."

This is another beatitude with a promise attached. If you develop a pure heart, you will *'see'* God. Not literally, but with the 'eyes' of your heart.

The heart of the issue is the issue of the heart. God only ever, always, looks at the heart. At our motive for doing things.

Motives. Interesting word. Motive – our *impulsion* for what we do.

Interesting to get real with our self sometimes and ask just what is my motive for doing this?

We need to get more and more real like the Skin Horse in the story of the Velveteen Rabbit.[1]

REAL. Done with hiding behind masks; trying to create an impression that we are something we are not.

Anything resonating there?

The world is full of them, the church, too...
Those who are part of the body, part of the church, who do not realise who they are and Whose they are. They are still posturing like the world to gain the recognition and approval they already have.

They are Royalty. But they don't know it or don't believe it. It has passed them by completely and they are still striving to impress; first themselves, then others.

Exhausting.

So being pure in heart means pure in motive. Not having a hidden agenda and being real. It all goes together.

What you believe in your heart is what you *really* believe.

It is not what you think, but what is in your heart and out of *that* you will speak.

> *"For out of the abundance of the heart the mouth speaks."* (Matthew 12: 34).

The scriptures have this way of finding us out, don't they?

We can fool some of the people some of the time. We can fool ourselves too, but we cannot fool God any of the time.

Good to keep that in mind.

Note

1. 'The Original Velveteen Rabbit' Margery Williams, p 10 Egmont UK Ltd. 2004

13

Out of the heart come

We have not finished with this yet.

> *"The things that come out of a person's mouth come from the heart, and these defile them. For out of the heart come evil thoughts – murder, adultery, sexual immorality, theft, false testimony, slander."* (Matthew 15:17-20 NIV).

Whether we recognise it or not, *'The poison of asps is under our tongue'* (Romans 3:13 KJV).

James has much to say about the tongue too, and the problems it can cause. Of course, it has its roots in the heart. That is the seat of our problems. All of them.

Purity of heart is something we need to seek after. It is characterised by the absence of bitterness and resentment, anger, blame and criticism.

You may have a problem with your temper; you have a short fuse and everybody knows it – they have perfected the art of walking on eggshells when they are around you. You cannot always help what you feel, but you *can* control what comes out of your mouth and how you speak and act.

Purity of heart is purity of motive. You speak from a place of purity of thought. Why?

Simply because you are sold out to God.

You will not allow anything that would affect that relationship to have life in you. So you find yourself apologising to Him for your thought life and what you say and how you act in an unguarded moment, and He does the rest. He transforms your heart so that it is pure.

Everything is relational.

It is not a form of godliness that denies the power. This is godliness worked in through your relationship with the Almighty by His power. Day after day after day as you yield yourself up to Him and eventually become His love slave.

What you think about God, therefore, is the single most important thing in your life. This whole thing revolves around how you see Him.

His Majesty.

How you think of Him. What you think of Him.

How much of Him you want in your life. And how much you allow Him to have of you.

That is the sum of our journey.

He is all you will ever need. That is how you get to see Him.

Something to think about today, eh?

14

It is incremental

Our next beatitude is:

> *"Blessed are the peacemakers, for they will be called children of God."* (Matthew 5:9 NIV).

Isn't that lovely? We all want to be peacemakers.

It is at this point we need to remind ourselves that the beatitudes build on one another. They are incremental. They describe the *progression* we are meant to make in the Christian life and walk.

We find the same thing in:

> *His divine power has given us everything we need for a godly life through our knowledge of him who called us by his own glory and goodness. Through these he has given us his very great and precious promises, so that through them you may participate in the divine nature, having escaped the corruption in the world caused by evil desires.*

For this very reason, make every effort to add to your faith goodness; and to goodness, knowledge; and to knowledge, self-control; and to self-control, perseverance; and to perseverance, godliness; and to godliness, mutual affection; and to mutual affection, love. For if you possess these qualities in increasing measure, they will keep you from being ineffective and unproductive in your knowledge of our Lord Jesus Christ. (2 Peter 1:3-8 NIV).

Peter shows us that there is only one way to live a godly life and that is through increasing our knowledge of the Lord Jesus Christ, who has already given us His divine power to make all this possible.

He has made us promises, but they are not automatically ours. We have a responsibility here. We need to possess these qualities in increasing measure in order to stop us from being ineffective and unproductive.

In this regard we can be our own worst enemy. If we tend to give up easily; not push through; condemn ourselves; huff, puff, complain, withdraw and generally have a negative outlook on life, we will end up being just what we do not want to be; ineffective and unproductive.

Remember all scripture is God breathed and is useful for teaching, rebuking, correcting and training in righteousness. (2 Timothy 3:16).

We come to peace with a promise attached – that we shall be called the children of God.

We are harbingers (forerunners, messengers, heralds) of peace, not confusion, strife, discord, argument, rebellion, refusal, stubbornness, recalcitrance, obstinacy, or childishness. Peace.

Paul says we need to have our feet shod with it. Except we make peace within ourselves *first*, we cannot hope to take it to others.

Jesus, during the storm on the lake (Mark 4: 39) spoke from His own inner well of peace. He did not call it out of the atmosphere and down onto the lake like a cowpat, if you are American, please read 'cow pie' here.

It came from His peace with God and with Himself and those around Him. Gaining and maintaining peace must be a priority for us.

Peace with ourselves, peace with God and following that will come peace with all men. Lovely stuff.

"I'll have some of that" I hear you say. You need to know this then – it is always worth reading the small print!

All this is conditional. Conditional on your co-operating with His divine power that will bring it about. It isn't a cowpat; it is not going to drop from a great height on you. It is not impartation or quick prayer but choices, your hard-nosed choices, in the difficult situations of life.

You are going to have to work at this thing. It is spelled e.f.f.o.r.t.

Thy Kingdom Come

Crisis to process. And choices.

Stick with the programme because we will have to come back to the business of acting against our natural selves again and again, to ensure that our peace level rises incrementally.

This could be a steep learning curve for some of us who are used to allowing that old black dog to have its way all the time with never a thought of controlling it.

Making choices to kill the beastie within. We are going to have to put that thing on a starvation diet and then some.

We will have to start agreeing with God and acting in accordance with what He is saying to us, not just making a mental assent and living in the land of wishful thinking. We are developing a backbone not a wishbone.

Character which influences. Ready?

Could you just check your footwear again please? You are not wearing carpet slippers are you? Because you are going to need to be properly shod for the climb that is ahead of us.

I will just wait here while you have a look.

See you next time.

15

Christian City

There is a modern-day allegory by one Robert Burnell.[1] It tells the tale of one man's desire to reach the City of God but first he stumbles across Christian City that he mistakes for the City of God.

In Christian City, the people have no idea what he is talking about when he asks the way to the City of God. Christian City has a mega-church on every corner; everyone carries a bible and goes around shouting 'hallelujah' at every available opportunity. They are all very, very busy, but there is no desire after the City of God. They are hardly aware that it exists.

The man nervously embarks on a journey striking off up a nearby mountain. Finding few travelling with him; he misses the way and even ends up back in Christian City, because he followed a crowd who appeared to be led by someone who knew where they were going.

It is a sad and salutary tale and it is only by much tribulation that he eventually arrives at his destination.

One thing I have asked from the Lord, that I shall seek: That I may dwell in the house of the Lord all the days of my life, to behold the beauty of the Lord and to meditate in His temple. (Psalm 27:4 NASB).

One thing I have asked, that shall I seek.

We need to know our destination on this journey. The beating heart of God, and we need to set our hearts to find Him. Match His intention with ours. Determine.

One thing... *that* I shall seek... Why?

There is no other stream. He and He alone is the source and the fulfilment of your life. He is the Alpha and the Omega. Without Him there is nothing.

We ended last time checking our footwear as we realised that Jesus is serious about all this and we found that to be a peacemaker we will probably have to make some serious mid-course corrections one way and another.

We needed to check our feet and our footwear. Feet have to do with destiny and victory – where and how you place them.

The wonderful promise of this beatitude is that we will be called *'the children of God'*. If we possess His grace and truth, His nature, in increasing amounts, people will know they have encountered the Living God when we are with them, and they will call us His offspring, His children.

Children are teachable, mouldable, and trusting. Qualities we will need to develop as we travel this road together to the City of God. That is where we are headed.

That is where understanding and walking in our destiny and identity won for us by Jesus on the Cross will take us.

We will not be unfruitful, unproductive or ineffective, if we understand we are back at school, in the School of the Spirit to be precise, and we are on a steep learning curve.

We do not know it you see. We really do not.

If we think we have got everything buttoned up, we are in for a few unpleasant surprises as things do not turn out as we expected.

Maybe we have lived too long in Christian City and God is urging us to move house which will mean decluttering and jettisoning a lot of things we considered to be precious; unlearning and relearning what it means to live life as a citizen of a different heavenly Kingdom, where love is the key.

The alternative is to settle in Christian City.

You choose which one you will have. *'As for me and my house, we will serve the Lord.'* Joshua said. (Joshua 24:14-15)

I am on my way to the City of God. How about you? Have you made your choice yet?

Note

1. 'Escape from Christendom', Robert Burnell

16

Where are you living

What about it beloved. Are you living in Christian City? Or are you seeking the City of God?

You will know if you are seeking the latter. It will mean you no longer insist on having things your way; on being first, best and right. You are happy to admit you are wrong. You have ceased rebellion against Him. Stopped justifying yourself. Stopped excusing yourself. You have recognised and admitted the pride within. You are choosing to take the lower place.

> *Dying with Jesus by death reckoned mine,*
> *Living with Jesus a new life divine,*
> *Looking to Jesus 'til glory doth shine,*
> *Moment by moment, O Lord, I am Thine...*[1]

They knew a thing or two those saints of the 19th and 20th centuries.

Without realising it we have lost so much of the Creator/ creature relationship in our present day. We are living in Christian City and we are not even aware of it.

Holiness and sanctification are words we can barely spell, let alone live. God is not life to us, but an adjunct to it. A means to an end. A passport to heaven. An add on. Our Life assurance – eternal life assurance.

He is not the Creator to whom we give honour and to Whom we defer in all things. He is not the *centre* of our existence. We are all about *'what's in it for me'.*

I tell you, I sense a change in the wind, that Father is saying *'Beloved, this is My time, My season'.*

The fulness of what this means has not yet been fully revealed, but one thing it does say is that our self-centred, self-referential lifestyles, are about to be shaken, in order that we become God-centred again in our approach to life and everything that pertains to it.

His Kingdom is coming. Our excuses will no longer hold up. We will have to stand up and be counted.

When you visit a foreign country if you unwittingly break their law, pleading ignorance will not help you; you will be taken to court and sentence will be passed.

In the Old Testament there was something called *'the sin of ignorance'* which needed to be confessed in order for the people to stay in fellowship with God. (Numbers 15:24-29).

He knew the people did not know or understand, so He made provision for that. But they had to confess, agree with Him, that they were in ignorance and in error.

It is good for us to get used to confessing it too because we do not know and we are in a time when we cannot justify our ignorance any longer.

> *In the past God overlooked such ignorance, but now he commands all people everywhere to repent.* (Acts 17:30 NIV).

There is a way in which we excuse our humanity, our sinfulness; by saying that we did not *know* that God expected something more of us.

There is a way in which we expect to be continuously excused because He loves us but conveniently forget that God disciplines those He loves; and chastens those He receives as sons. (Hebrews 12:6).

Time after time, after time we refuse correction, justify our behaviour.

Remorse is when we do not make any effort to change when we are found out.

Repentance is a change of heart and mind and results in changed behaviour.

Here comes a moment of inconvenient enlightenment. You are a *new creation*. The old has gone, the new has come. You cannot spend all day talking to a corpse.

In the time that is upon us, we are discovering we do not know anything, so the low position of humbling ourselves and admitting our poverty of spirit and ignorance is here.

We must become humble and accept the mercy He extends to us in our ignorance and not go to Him loudly protesting our innocence because it just will not work any longer.

We have to admit we do not know. We do not know how to love and we don't know how to live. We do not know how to give in this new Kingdom.

But we are expected to acknowledge the fact and become teachable, mouldable and correctable. If we do not, we prove yet again what out-and-out rebels we are.

There is one more result from continuing in this sort of pattern and that is, time runs out for us. Because we have refused correction so often; pleaded we do not understand for the last time; we disqualify ourselves from the high calling He has on our lives. We have settled for something less than His best.

We have done it and there is a law involved which we will examine tomorrow.

We do not lose our salvation and He does not love us any the less. What happens is we lose our ability to be useful in the Kingdom and therefore forfeit our rewards because we have run out of time.

We used our time unwisely in procrastination and complaint, never actually addressing what He was showing us, and He has to set us aside. Pass us over and go on to someone who will do what He asks, when He asks and how He asks.

Resonate with anyone? If it does, you know what to do.

Note

1. D W Whittle, Redemption Hymnal number 384.

17

Laws

Some of you may be reeling from the thought that it is possible to disqualify ourselves. That there were still rules (read laws) in place. You really did not understand that God was so serious about all this.

When God puts a law in our path beloved, we have a choice. Your choice at this point will empower or disempower you. Write that down and pin it all round your house!

It is absolutely vital you understand the consequences of your choices.

We need to acknowledge and bow the knee to the fact that He placed laws in His universe. Gravity is one that easily springs to mind. That is a natural law. Drop something and it gravitates to the earth, it doesn't float off into the atmosphere. We understand that and we live with it. We don't even think about it, it is so much a part of life.

Spiritually there are laws too. The law of sowing and reaping is a good example. You cannot sow one crop and reap another. You can sow wheat and expect potatoes if you like, but wheat is what you will get.

If you sow discord, strife, anger, bitterness, resentment, criticism, rebellion and independence, guess what you will get back?

Laws, rules are part of life.

Allow me to remind you, Father's primary objective is to make you like His Son. That is His agenda for your life. Everything in your life will be to that one end. So, He needs you to align yourself with Him in every aspect of your life, not just those that suit you.

We must be careful what we sow. Continuously sowing resentment, rebellion and independence will not bring you into a harvest of righteousness.

God is not surprised or dismayed by our behaviour, He knew what He was getting. But He does challenge us to change; give us the means to do so and then He watches.

Rather like a coach watching the runners and seeing those who are trying to take a short cut, He is overseeing the whole field. He is not watching to see if you *win*, but *how* you run. Whether you run according to His rules, His laws, His regulations.

He is the Judge you see. He will hand out the prizes at the end of the race.

Paul wrote on the subject:

We all know that when there's a race, all the runners bolt for the finish line, but only one will take the prize. When you run, run for the prize! Athletes in training are very strict with themselves, exercising self-control over desires, and for what? For a wreath that soon withers or is crushed or simply forgotten. That is not our race. We run for the crown that we will wear for eternity. So I don't run aimlessly. I don't let my eyes drift off the finish line. When I box, I don't throw punches in the air. I discipline my body and make it my slave so that after all this, after I have brought the gospel to others, I will still be qualified to win the prize. (1 Corinthians 9:24-27 The Voice).

Self-control and desires. This is very up front and personal and it affects each individual runner. They must run according to the rules or they may be disqualified, losing both their crown and their reward.

The Greek word for disqualify means to be *'ordered to stand aside'*. By our behaviour, our lifestyle, we render ourselves ineligible for the reward at the end of the race.

We can be half-hearted, saying "yes" whilst in our hearts we are saying "no". So we do not put our best into what we have been called to do or we do it but grudgingly.

We have already seen that it is possible to lose our inheritance by trading it or despising it. Now Paul talks about the eternal prize and reward in a similar way. He tells us we cannot live sloppy and undisciplined lives if we want to win the race of life and gain the crown.

Self-control and discipline are both words we do not like, but God does not shrink from using them. He knows what chocolate soldiers, what weekend warriors we are. We will try to cut across the park if we can.

He sent prophets to Israel for hundreds of years to try to get their attention to get them to shape up, but they never heeded Him. Nag, nag, nag, was all they ever said. They did not discern the voice of God speaking through the prophets. They thought they were just men who were nagging.

They are still in the fifth cycle of discipline. (Leviticus 26 or go to www.psalm131.com and search for 'The Five Cycles of Discipline' for a fuller understanding).

And I am nagging. Nag, nag, nag. Time to straighten up and fly right side up.

God's rules, His laws, are designed to reveal your rebellion, resentment and independence (among other things) and bring about a change in your behaviour.

Set them all aside and run as though your life and eternal reward depends upon it, because it does.

You will never regret *that* choice.

18

Persecution for righteousness sake

"Blessed are those who have been persecuted for the sake of righteousness, for theirs is the kingdom of heaven. Blessed are you when people insult you and persecute you, and falsely say all kinds of evil against you because of Me. Rejoice and be glad, for your reward in heaven is great; for in the same way they persecuted the prophets who were before you." (Matthew 5:10-12 NASB).

Here is a big one.

Many Christians think they are being persecuted for their faith when it is their *behaviour* that is attracting it.

Going where you have not been sent and doing what you have not been asked by God to do can attract persecution from the world, even if you think you are doing God a favour.

There are other ways in which we can attract persecution from believers. This scripture does not say blessed are those who are being objectionable or who are having a hard time, but blessed are those who are persecuted because of *Him* in their hunger and thirst to be like Him.

Living a life that is God-centred will attract all kinds of negatives from fellow Christians. If you seek to walk as Jesus did you will attract the same warfare as He did. You will be persecuted, and that by your own.

What are you going to do with that? How are you going to behave when a fellow believer persecutes you?

Will you make a defence? Will you sort them out? Give them a fistful of five-fold ministry?

There is only one way if you are truly set on following Him and that is to respond in the *opposite* spirit to that which is coming against you.

When you are reviled, you bless. When you are criticised and blamed, you bless. When you are held up to ridicule, you bless. When you are attacked, you do not defend yourself, you leave the Lord to defend or vindicate you; meanwhile, you bless.

It's going to be a hard road. The road less travelled. Many will desire to walk it; the idea is appealing; the reality – hard.

Pleasing God rather than man will get you into all sorts of trouble. But you will be following the saints who went before:

For am I now seeking the favour of men, or of God? Or am I striving to please men? If I were still trying to please men, I would not be a bond-servant of Christ. (Galatians 1:10 NASB).

Paul makes it abundantly clear that to be a bondservant, a love slave of Jesus, will mean you are not seeking to please man.

A love slave. That is what we are talking about. Not a believer, not just a follower, but a disciple, a love slave, who seeks to emulate the Master in everything.

He did not return reviling for reviling, but blessing; He did not lift up His voice in the streets; He suffered in silence; and in the last analysis He said:

"Father, forgive them, they don't know what they are doing." (Luke 23:34).

Persecution for the sake of righteousness.

It is an issue of the heart. That could separate the men from the boys right there.

I leave you to think about it because there is a little more. There is another verse to come.

19
More

There is a second part to this beatitude about persecution:

"Blessed are you when people insult you and persecute you, and falsely say all kinds of evil against you because of Me. Rejoice and be glad, for your reward in heaven is great; for in the same way they persecuted the prophets who were before you." (Matthew 5:10-12 NASB).

One of the things hardest to endure is people speaking about you *falsely* and not defending yourself. They are not speaking about you with reason, but falsely. Speaking behind your back or even to your face; criticising you in public and holding you up as an example of what not to be.

You are being falsely accused. Insulted. Your good is being evil spoken of.

Time to rejoice:

If you are insulted for the name of Christ, blessed are you, for the Spirit of glory and of God rests upon you. (1 Peter 4:14 NASB).

We have to ask ourselves what would Jesus do in this situation? It is a wonderful opportunity to turn the other cheek and respond in the opposite spirit; to start qualifying for the reward.

Many of us like to wear the slogan *'what would Jesus do?'* around our wrists, not unlike the phylacteries the Jews wore to remind themselves of God's commands. Unfortunately like those Jews, it does not get any further because we do not actually *ask* Him what He wants to do or say in any given circumstance. It is just another Christian fad.

I have seen plenty of those come and go over the years. *This* has to *become flesh* on us. Not just outwardly, but inwardly.

Our hearts need to change, and come to the place where there is no desire to retaliate or pay back like for like: *"I know something about you too, pal."*

It has to become a way of life, not reviling when you are reviled. Itis called death on the instalment plan.

Paul knew about it, he said *"I die daily"*. (1 Corinthians 15:31).

You will get plenty of practice in dying to yourself if you really seek to walk *'godly in Christ Jesus'* but it's a joy. It is what the Christian walk is all about – learning to be like Him, being conformed to His image and following God's plan for our lives. You will be given plenty of opportunities to keep your mouth shut and your heart open every day.

Some of us do not say much, and perhaps pride ourselves on our silence, but that does not mean nothing is going on inside. Some of the most bitter and mean-spirited people are those who keep pursed lips and silence.

> *Their throat is an open tomb; With their tongues they have practiced deceit; The poison of asps is under their lips.* (Romans 3:13).

It is speaking primarily of the unbeliever. It talks of the *'poison of asps'* under the tongue; they speak from their fallen nature. Or a believer who is still walking after the flesh, the old man, is in exactly the same position.

Out of the abundance of their heart comes the bitterness, the angst and the gall that is stored up there. Spend some time in their company and you will know what is in their heart because it comes straight out of their mouths. The reason being they are not making will choices to live from the new heart. They are still feeding that black dog.

I said at the beginning I would show you the way out of bondage to the flesh life, I also said I did not think many of you would actually choose to take it. We have just looked at a couple of exits that could cause major problems in the *'defend, justify, and excuse'* departments.

So, question, just how is it working out for you?

20

Eternal rewards

We cannot leave this without looking at the reward there is for those who rejoice when they are persecuted for His sake and the cause of righteousness.

> *"Rejoice and be glad, for your reward in heaven is great; for in the same way they persecuted the prophets who were before you."* (Matthew 5:12).

Great reward is there in heaven for those who will both enjoy and endure the cost of being a disciple. Who walk the talk. Follow the Master and rejoice.

We have seen we can bring great suffering on ourselves and create difficulties which are totally unnecessary, because we have some foolish notions about witnessing or testifying because it is done in a spirit of self-righteousness. We really do call it down on our own heads.

We do not want to be found to be persecuted for a 'cause' either. There is such a subtle line here; it totally depends on our motives and where we are living from. If we are testifying or witnessing to further a cause, even if we think that cause is Christ, persecution may well come but the reward will not.

It is true that some preach Christ out of envy and rivalry, but others out of goodwill. The latter do so out of love, knowing that I am put here for the defence of the gospel. (Philippians 1:15 NIV).

The key is found here:

Anyone who wants to live all out for Christ is in for a lot of trouble; there's no getting around it. (2 Timothy 3:12 MSG).

It is all about living *all out* for Jesus. Making Him central to your existence. Loving Him from the love He gives us and doing what He asks when He asks.

What you think about God is the single most important thing in your life? Time to rejoice and be exceedingly glad if you are becoming God-centred, because great is your reward in heaven.

This poses several questions for us:

- What *are* we living for and from?
- The here and now or what is to come?
- Where are we living from, Heaven or earth?

We do have to sort these out because we will either be striving for one thing or the other. To be like Christ, or have our own way.

There is a sharp division. If my outlook is governed by Whose I am, where I am going and what awaits me there, I will be heavenly minded. I will be seeking God with everything that is within me, and to be like Christ and see His Kingdom come in my life.

If am focussed on things below, on the earthly and material world, I will not be storing up treasure in heaven, I'll be in the moth, rust and thieves division.

Endure or enjoy? It was by enduring the Cross, despising the shame, Jesus saw the joy that was set before Him –

Stay focused on Jesus, who designed and perfected our faith. He endured the cross and ignored the shame of that death because He focused on the joy that was set before Him; and now He is seated beside God on the throne, a place of honour. Consider the life of the One who endured such personal attacks and hostility from sinners so that you will not grow weary or lose heart. (Hebrews 12:1-3 The Voice).

It is food for thought isn't it?

The rubber is really going to start hitting the road shortly.

21

Salt

From this point on Jesus begins to expand on the things He has said, beginning by likening believers to salt.

From Matthew 5:1-11, Jesus had spelled out the conditions for inheriting the Kingdom; being comforted and filled and seeing God; one building incrementally on the other. Now He begins to open up in detail what He is talking about and from this point on begins to teach them in depth.

He starts by likening His disciples to something very well-known and precious to them – salt.

> *"Let me tell you why you are here. You're here to be salt-seasoning that brings out the God-flavours of this earth. If you lose your saltiness, how will people taste godliness? You've lost your usefulness and will end up in the garbage."* (Matthew 5:13 MSG).

Salt. Purifies, preserves, cleanses and seasons.

If we are of value we are said to be *'worth our salt'*. It is where we get our word 'salary' from: we are worth our salt, our payment, wage, salary. Salt was paid as a wage in ancient times. In China its value was second only to gold, so important was it to purify, preserve, cleanse and season.

Wounds were washed with a solution of it to cleanse them; meat and fish were preserved by using it; stains could be removed by its application; and it was used to season food in cooking.

That makes us pretty useful too as we are likened to salt. No wonder Jesus says if you have lost your quality of saltiness, you will end up being thrown on the heap, or trodden underfoot. (Matthew 5:13)

Paul said we could be disqualified because we had lost our usefulness, our preserving, cleansing, flavouring qualities. (1 Corinthians 9:27)

Ties together somehow. But then it would. It has the same author. The Holy Spirit.

Sometimes salt was adulterated, though, by being mixed with another ingredient which caused it to lose its effectiveness.

Mixture. We are warned against mixture. God does not like it. Light and darkness for instance. Black and white.

Sometimes we can be accused of being *'too black and white'*, when in fact there are two kingdoms at work, the one Light and other darkness.

Paul warns against it:

Do not be bound together with unbelievers; for what partnership have righteousness and lawlessness, or what fellowship has light with darkness? (2 Corinthians 6:14).

What we are talking about here effectively is holiness.

Pursue peace with all people, and holiness, without which no one will see the Lord. (Hebrews 12:14).

There is a way in which we have to separate ourselves, without separating ourselves if that makes sense; we are in the world but not of it. We live in two realities – the world and heaven. We need to be separate in the way we see things, the way we perceive situations and the way we look at people.

This means our value system must change. We can no longer have any enemies for instance.

There is just one enemy so far as we are concerned, his name is Satan. People are not our enemies, ever.

That is going to turn our thinking upside down right there, as we begin to put into practice what Jesus is saying, responding in the opposite spirit when we are wrongly accused and our good is evil spoken of.

Could take a lifetime. But then it is meant to; that is our journey.

22

And light

"You are the light of the world. A town built on a hill cannot be hidden. Neither do people light a lamp and put it under a bowl. Instead they put it on its stand, and it gives light to everyone in the house." (Matthew 5:14-15 NIV).

This is where the Sermon begins to bite.

We are now expected to walk the talk; live what we say we believe; not just carry a bible, live it. Show by our lifestyle we now have a different set of values. Act like a believer, not just talk about being one. Be an example, a good one.

It is going to hit us right where we live. Where the rubber hits the road as they say.

As His own, Jesus talks to us and teaches us, because He has a purpose for us in this present darkness.

We need to be straightened out from our own crookedness first in order that we may be an example and, in turn, be able to help others become straight. As someone has said, we are born bent. We are weak, twisted and deceitful people, but He loves us with a passion; a passion that will not leave us where we are but seeks to transform us into His likeness; to make us straight again.

We are not saved *by* good works, but in order that we may *do* good works. So first He must straighten us out before we can be of use to anyone; before we can be a light to others in a dark place. We need to be heavenly minded enough to be some earthly good.

We live, we now discover, in two realities, not one. The reality of Heaven must touch us in order that we, in turn, may touch earth with the power of God.

We are His witnesses, His ambassadors by our character, our conduct and our influence.

By saying that we are both salt and light, Jesus is showing that there is something both decaying and dark about the world around us. In one role we are going to act as a preservative, in the other we will bring light, illumination.

Jesus always speaks to what we are *becoming* not what we are. He always addresses us present/future and in this scripture, He tells His hearers how He sees them: *"You are both salt and light"*.

It may not match with where they are (or we are for that matter) right now, but He is prophetic. All the time, He speaks to what He sees we can become.

Suddenly *'Be holy as I am holy'* becomes a distinct possibility. Are you up for that?

Stick with the programme then, because you are being transformed from one degree of glory to another by the Spirit of the Lord. (2 Corinthians 3:18).

Isn't *that* good news?

23

Let it shine

"In the same way, let your light shine before others, that they may see your good deeds and glorify your Father in heaven." (Matthew 5:16)

Now Jesus switches to your 'good deeds' and links them to the attributes of salt and light by using *"in the same way"*.

Your knowledge of Him and the Gospel –

"Everyone who does evil hates the light, and will not come into the light for fear that their deeds will be exposed. But whoever lives by the truth comes into the light, so that it may be seen plainly that what they have done has been done in the sight of God." (John 3:20-21 NIV).

People of light cannot help but make a difference. Their *'deeds'* are in the sight of God and they know it; everything is for an audience of One.

But light is repugnant to the darkness. We said at the beginning of this study that character begets conduct; conduct begets influence and influence is shown in deeds of goodness, mercy and kindness to those around us. Character is in the fruit of the Spirit evident in our lives. One thing follows sequentially upon the other.

This is why what we *think* is so important, because what follows is what we do, our deeds. If our thought life is pure, then our lives will have some semblance of purity. Our motive will be good and it will show.

The thought, it is said, is father to the deed.

It will quickly become apparent that we no longer watch what we used to or want to join others in what they do. We lack the desire to get involved any more, we have no taste for it, no appetite.

We *were* like that, now we are like this:

> *Do you not know that the unrighteous will not inherit the kingdom of God? Do not be deceived. Neither fornicators, nor idolaters, nor adulterers, nor homosexuals, nor sodomites, nor thieves, nor covetous, nor drunkards, nor revilers, nor extortioners will inherit the kingdom of God. And such **were** some of you. But you **were** washed, but you **were** sanctified, but you **were** justified in the name of the Lord Jesus and by the Spirit of our God.* (1 Corinthians 6:9-11 NIV emphasis added).

We were like that but we have lost the taste for *'drunkenness and carousing'* as the King James has it; or for *'adultery and covetousness',* for example.

This is where persecution can arise. The light does not draw attention to itself; it illuminates what is there.

For us, it will highlight or illuminate, the work of God in our lives and through our lives, and in that way the Father is glorified in us and through us.

He is not glorified, however, when we draw attention to ourselves and our good deeds. The Pharisees did that for one reason – for men to see. We are exhorted not to be like them.

When we get Matthew 6:33, seeking only His Kingdom, we will begin to understand how all this fits together. Putting Jesus and His Kingdom first simply and effortlessly removes our appetite for the things of the world and its approval.

He comes first.

24

Saved by grace alone

'Saved, by grace alone!
This is all my plea;
Jesus died for all mankind
and Jesus died for me.'[1]

Before we leave the issue of salt and light we need to reinforce the fact that we are not saved by works, but by grace alone.

Good deeds are often translated *'good works'*, *'good things we do'* and *'the good we do'*. All are manifestations of the fact that we are people of light who live in the light.

Everything we are starts with us being broken. How we hate that word. Broken. He breaks up our fallow ground and our stony hearts.

But brokenness is essential for a life poured out as Jesus describes it in His sermon. Brokenness is what the Holy Spirit works in us and through us.

He replaces our meanness with His kindness. Our rebellion with His meekness.

Life in the Spirit is about displacement and replacement. He takes out all that does not look like Jesus and replaces it with Himself. Cool.

Paul says it another way:

> *Saving is all his idea, and all his work. All we do is trust him enough to let him do it. It's God's gift from start to finish! We don't play the major role. If we did, we'd probably go around bragging that we'd done the whole thing! No, we neither make nor save ourselves. God does both the making and saving. He creates each of us by Christ Jesus to join him in the work he does, the good work he has gotten ready for us to do, work we had better be doing.* (Ephesians 2:7-10 MSG).

Good works do not precede our conversion, they follow it. They flow from the regenerated spirit, through the soul, to the body that performs them. Good works are a test of whether or not we are living in the Beatitudes.

If we are, we can begin to trace our growth through them. As we have said, they are incremental, they build one upon the other.

Our light shows other people that Jesus is the Way the Truth and the Life. Our light is like the sun, it has warmth; it draws; it welcomes people to bask in it.

It is inclusive, not exclusive. It lets them know that no one will be rejected or cast aside as worthless. It listens, it leans, it lifts.

Whether we like it or not, the world is watching us and we may be the only Bible they will ever read.

We declare we are Christians, Christ-ones, and they are looking to us to see:

- what our standards are;
- what our values are;
- whether our lives line up with what we profess;
- how we react in a crisis;
- whether we do have Someone who is out of this world that supports, nourishes and provides for us;
- whether we do have confidence in this Supreme Being of beings whom we say we know.

Our light is not hidden, it is shining before men for all to see, and so what Jesus is saying here is *'live in such a way I can be seen in you and through you'.* John the Baptist summed it up:

"He must increase, I must decrease." (John 3:30 NASB).

And Jesus, His classic one-liner did the same –

"Without Me you can do nothing." (John 15:5).

All is grace and changed government.

Note
1. *'Grace! 'Tis a charming sound'.* P Doddridge, Redemption Hymnal, number 325.

25

Changing our centre

Recentering.

Strange word that, recentering.

What I am getting at is changing our centre. Changing the pivot of our life. Confessing the changed ownership. That it is no longer your life, but His through you to be lived.

Currently it maybe you calling the shots. I, me and mine. We need to change it, to Jesus at the centre. Him. Central.

It is a governmental transfer. Remember that is what happened when you underwent baptism. You have been baptised, fully immersed, haven't you?

It is a foundational requirement: *'arise and be baptised'*, you need this because before we can go on. He must be enthroned in your life. You need to agree with the transfer of power.

He must be allowed to rule and reign. He will never force

or coerce you. He will only ever present you with a choice.

But present you He will. With choices that is. They will either advance or retard your growth. You will either grow better or bitter. Choice is yours.

You must keep in mind that without Him you can do nothing of eternal value, nothing that will carry a reward on that day. The choice is entirely yours. Believer, follower, disciple; you get to choose all the time.

Every now and again that issue comes up doesn't it? As we are going to look very shortly at some life changing demands that are made on us in this teaching on the Kingdom, we need to sit down and count the cost again.

Everything.

That is the cost if you want to go the full distance. All your time, all your money and all your resources. Your whole self. It is all going to come under the Divine microscope. The way you currently spend your time, money and resources.

Imagine the dialogue:

> *"Lord, I have time"*
> *"I know, it is the way you **spend it** I want to talk about..."*

Everything needs to come under the benevolent dictatorship of the indwelling Holy Spirit. He does not indwell you simply so you can move in the gift He gives you beloved, or speak in tongues at will. No, when He comes, He comes with the express intention of taking over.

Time for a rethink again? I will leave you to do that then.

26

Repetition

We probably need to spend a few moments redefining what the Kingdom of God coming in our lives will look like.

In the parable of the sower, the seed broadcast was good, but it got snatched away until the returns were 30, 60 and rarely 100-fold.

You know the farmers saying: *'four seeds in the hole, one for rook, one for crow, one to rot and one to grow'*.

It could imply that we will need to hear this teaching at least four times before it takes root because it can get snatched away.

We do need to see what we are getting ourselves into because the way will not get broader but narrower. We will get squeezed through some tight places as Jesus explains what He wants from us and then makes it real in our experience, as we walk in the new nature He has imputed to us.

One of the little words we continually see Jesus used was *'if'*.

'If,' perhaps you will, perhaps you will not. Either way He won't love you any the less.

Take Up the Cross and Follow Him

> *Then Jesus said to His disciples, "If anyone desires to come after Me, let him deny himself, and take up his cross, and follow Me."* (Matthew 16:24).

And in **The Message** version it comes out like this:

> *Then Jesus went to work on his disciples. "Anyone who intends to come with me has to let me lead. You're not in the driver's seat; I am. Don't run from suffering; embrace it. Follow me and I'll show you how. Self-help is no help at all. Self-sacrifice is the way, my way, to finding yourself, your true self. What kind of deal is it to get everything you want but lose yourself? What could you ever trade your soul for?".*

The Kingdom is upside down; we die to live, give to receive and lose to gain. Does not compute with the natural man!

The Sermon on the Mount talks of life lived by the *Spirit of God,* not the natural life lived by the unregenerate nature. The only way we can do this thing is by allowing the Spirit to have sway; letting Him take over more and more of our lives until He has complete control.

This is why many commentators have said the Sermon on the Mount is for the heavenly Kingdom and not for now. What they have missed is that you will not have any opportunities to turn the other cheek, go the extra mile, or bless those who curse you when you get there! All will be bliss.

No. This is for the here and now; for whosoever will; *provided* they are filled with the Spirit.

Which brings us nicely to the next issue we have not addressed. Baptism in the Holy Spirit.

Being baptised in the Holy Spirit is just the same as water baptism. You are plunged into Him and He comes in His fullness into you. The water is in the bottle and the bottle is in the water.

When He comes His intention is to take over. He has you, you do not have Him. He is gentle. He will never push, coerce or pressure you to do anything.

This same Spirit gave you free will and as we have seen it is really only free to step away from God, to rebel, when what it really needs is to learn is to lean into God and yield to Him. Therein lies the whole of our journey really, learning to *lean* –

Who is this coming up from the wilderness, leaning upon her beloved? (Song of Songs 8:5).

Leaning.

That is the whole of our journey encapsulated right there. From being self-sufficient and independent, to leaning the whole of our weight upon the Beloved and totally depending upon Him for everything; health, wealth, happiness.

Beryl Moore

The hardest thing in the world is letting go. Yielding.

How is it working out for you?

27

Receiving the gift

I do not want to leave you with a cliff-hanger. If you have not received the gift of the baptism in the Holy Spirit, and you desire to, all that is required is a seeking heart.

Some folks have the idea that if you are not baptised in the Spirit you are some sort of a second-class citizen; you surely are not. What has happened is that you have missed out on all Jesus promised and wants you to have. In John 20:22 we see the disciples receiving the new birth. Jesus is now the resurrected, risen Lord and He breathes resurrection *life* into them:

> *And when He had said this, He breathed on them, and said to them, "Receive the Holy Spirit".* (John 20:22).

They are now alive again, this time the inspiration is from above, not below.

> *But as many as received Him, to them He gave the right to become children of God, to those who believe in His name: who were born, not of blood, nor of the will of the flesh, nor of the will of man, but of God.* (John 1:12-13).

There are two distinct and separate experiences to the rebirth. The first when the risen Lord breathes resurrection life into them, just as He breathed into Adam in the garden. The second when having been told to wait in Jerusalem, the Spirit comes on them in *power* when they are all together and in one accord; to indwell and enable them to do what He has commissioned them to do.

> *When the Day of Pentecost had fully come, they were all with one accord in one place. And suddenly there came a sound from heaven, as of a rushing mighty wind, and it filled the whole house where they were sitting. Then there appeared to them divided tongues, as of fire, and one sat upon each of them. And they were all filled with the Holy Spirit and began to speak with other tongues, as the Spirit gave them utterance.* (Acts 2:1-3).

It is the Spirit who gives the utterance, the Spirit who endues them with power and the Spirit who does the work. Ours is simply to *yield* to His dominion, His agenda, His life within us. It is very important that we understand this or we will be living a life of constantly striving to get somewhere we are already.

He has done it all. We simply receive it. No more, no less. Done deal.

Conflict we will have though, because there are now two wills at work within us, like two cats in a bag. There is your natural will and the will of the Spirit and these two are at war with one another.

If you do not believe me, look at this:

Those who think they can do it on their own end up obsessed with measuring their own moral muscle but never get around to exercising it in real life. Those who trust God's action in them find that God's Spirit is in them – living and breathing God! Obsession with self in these matters is a dead end; attention to God leads us out into the open, into a spacious, free life. Focusing on the self is the opposite of focusing on God. Anyone completely absorbed in self ignores God, ends up thinking more about self than God. That person ignores who God is and what he is doing. And God isn't pleased at being ignored. (Romans 8:5-8 MSG).

And this:

Light Bearers

Therefore, my beloved, as you have always obeyed, not as in my presence only, but now much more in my absence, work out your own salvation with fear and trembling; for it is God who works in you both to will and to do for His good pleasure. (Philippians 2:12-14).

No longer two wills or two lives to be lived, but one: His through you. You no longer occupy the throne of your life, He does.

That is the reality of your Christian life and walk, the transformation process that takes you from crisis to process. When the Holy Spirit comes, He will speak of Jesus, our Bridegroom, and Coming King –

"The Helper will come – the Spirit, who reveals the truth about God and who comes from the Father. I will send him to you from the Father, and he will speak about me." (John 15:26 GNB).

His Majesty before whom every knee will bow.

How is it working out for you?

28

A Higher Place

The fulfilment of the law

> *Do not think that I have come to abolish the Law or the Prophets; I have not come to abolish them but to fulfil them. For truly I tell you, until heaven and earth disappear, not the smallest letter, not the least stroke of a pen, will by any means disappear from the Law until everything is accomplished. Therefore anyone who sets aside one of the least of these commands and teaches others accordingly will be called least in the kingdom of heaven, but whoever practises and teaches these commands will be called great in the kingdom of heaven. For I tell you that unless your righteousness surpasses that of the Pharisees and the teachers of the law, you will certainly not enter the kingdom of heaven.* (Matthew 5:14-20 NIV).

Now Jesus tells us that His *law* is still applicable in the Kingdom, but the way it works out is completely different. Now it is internal, not external.

Whether you keep it or not will be revealed in your life by

your attitudes and behaviours, your reactions or responses; your rebellion, resentment and independence. There will be no hiding place.

Your lifestyle will be the gospel you preach. Your light will shine, it is just a question of whether that light is darkness or not.

It will not be about an outward show of piety, form and religion, but relationship and the Holy Spirit's ministry of the interior.

"If you love Me, you will keep My commandments." (John 14:15)

You have changed both nation and law. The natural law has no effect in this Kingdom. *'If you love Me you will allow Me to make the changes necessary inside you to fully become a Kingdom citizen in order that you live a kingdom lifestyle.'*

Here it is fulfilled in one word – Love:

If I give everything I own to the poor and even go to the stake to be burned as a martyr, but I don't love, I've gotten nowhere. So, no matter what I say, what I believe, and what I do, I'm bankrupt without love.

Love never gives up.
Love cares more for others than for self.
Love doesn't want what it doesn't have.
Love doesn't strut,
Doesn't have a swelled head,
Doesn't force itself on others,

Thy Kingdom Come

Isn't always "me first,"
Doesn't fly off the handle,
Doesn't keep score of the sins of others,
Doesn't revel when others grovel,
Takes pleasure in the flowering of truth,
Puts up with anything,
Trusts God always,
Always looks for the best,
Never looks back,
But keeps going to the end.
Love never dies. (1 Corinthians 13:3-10 MSG).

We have entered the Kingdom where love is the key. The change inside when this Kingdom hits is radical. Nothing from the old fits.

From now on Jesus is going to keep repeating *'You have heard it said, but I say to you'* signifying there is a higher authority at work, and a higher place from which to live.

29

Thy Kingdom Come

"Thy will be done, Thy Kingdom come on earth as it is in heaven."

It seems to me that God is answering that prayer right now. We have prayed it time without number without realising what we are asking for; that His rule and reign should come in us first, and then on the earth in general.

He is answering us.

Wherever I look Christians are in deep water one way or the other and some, bless them, really do not understand what is happening.

Simply put, Father is giving you what you have asked for. He is bringing His Kingdom to bear on your life and the circumstances in which you find yourself are the evidence of this.

The proper response is thanksgiving:

Rejoice always, pray continually, give thanks in all circumstances; for this is God's will for you in Christ

*Jesus. Do not quench the Spirit. (*1 Thessalonians 5:16-19 NIV).

Do not quench the Spirit. We must be careful not to do this by our reactions. We don't want to be found to be in rebellion, resentment or declaring our independence from Him at this stage.

We may need to retrace our steps and look again at the analogy of the runner that Paul uses:

Do you not know that in a race all the runners run, but only one gets the prize? Run in such a way as to get the prize. Everyone who competes in the games goes into strict training. They do it to get a crown that will not last, but we do it to get a crown that will last forever. Therefore I do not run like someone running aimlessly; I do not fight like a boxer beating the air. No, I strike a blow to my body and make it my slave so that after I have preached to others, I myself will not be disqualified for the prize. (1 Corinthians 9:24-27).

Athletes train for the race. Paul describes it as strict training. They put aside everything else because they want to win the prize. It will mean denying themselves all sorts of things that would have otherwise have occupied their time and resources. They will often go on a strict diet and be found training in every available moment of spare time whilst others are enjoying themselves. They get ticked off with the coach from time to time too; he just keeps pushing them when they want to stop.

It is hard. But he and they are after something. Winning the prize. They're in it for the reward at the end, he wants them to receive it, so he pushes them to their limit.

Keep in mind what Father is doing is bringing about what we have asked for. He uses our life situations and circumstances to do this.

If you have asked for His Kingdom to come, that is what He will be fulfilling in your life. If you have asked for a gift, ditto. If you have a specific call this will be your training ground.

So look up and rejoice, you are being made fit for either the coming Kingdom or for the assignment He has given you. Either way you win. So please stop complaining.

No-one drifts to the top of the mountain. Would you please just check your footwear, you could find you are in carpet slippers again.

"Lay off Sarge!" Welcome to boot camp.

30

Training for reigning

Training for reigning, that is what is happening here as His Kingdom comes in our lives as a reality, not a pipe dream. As we find ourselves in God's version of boot camp.

He has a dream all right, but it is not the same as ours. He sees you mature and complete in His Son *now*. He sees you in the future and you look much better than you do right now.

Your journey is getting to that place; whether you agree with that or not; understand it or not. He is going to do this thing and He is going to bring you into maturity.

You see life with a cottage and roses around the door. A life of bliss here on earth perhaps or a ministry with you as the star?

He has another agenda. When we enter the Kingdom, we find ourselves under another government and that government will not let us go until it has established in us the things it purposes.

God is *fully* intentional towards you. He has a plan and that plan will not be thwarted. His will *for* you is about to become apparent *to* you.

He intends that you become through, crisis and process, like His Son. Your part is to make it easy, both for Him and you. *You* determine how difficult the path will be. You determine it by your co-operation (or lack of it) with Him.

He is fully committed to making you as like Himself as possible, in order that you will be a fit eternal companion for the King of Kings. This is not a *'pour on hot water and stir'* package.

God does not do instant, at least not very often and certainly not where character and conduct are concerned.

He could transform us by a word, but we would learn nothing of Him or ourselves if He did. We have to come to the place where we admit we are weak, foolish and deceitful people. We are intransigent and stubborn and in our natural self dwells no good thing.

He only ever speaks to the Jesus in us. The new life in us.

He wants you to enjoy this journey, not keep complaining and looking to see when you can get off.

To Him it is the journey that is important. To you it is the end result.

"I need patience and can I have it now, please." Sometimes

we don't even say *"please"*!

As we found out in the first book, *'The School of the Spirit',* God's ways are certainly not ours. So it behoves us to move our feet and change our minds because He surely is not going to change:

"*I the Lord change not.*" (Malachi 3:6 NIV).

But therein lies our security. He never, ever, changes the way He sees us and the way He thinks towards us. He always has good plans for us. For our ultimate good.

Everything He does is good, because He is good and He never, ever deals with sin in our lives, He only deals with us in righteousness.

Sin is dealt with. Yes, we do sin and miss the mark, and yes we do still need 1 John 1:9 from time to time. But as far as He is concerned He only ever deals with us in the completed work of His Son; in righteousness, which He is working into us.

He will not come to you in your pity party and poor me. He will only come to you in His Son.

That could be the reason for the silence right now. You are wailing and waiting in the wrong place – just a thought.

Beloved of God you are part of the army of God, you are a warrior bride, and it is time to take your place.

Subdue your flesh and walk the way of the Spirit.

31

Come up higher

I ended yesterday by talking about the army of God and the fact that we are part of a warrior bride whether we know it or not, whether we understand what that means, or not.

We are in a fight between God on the one hand and Satan on the other. Take heart beloved of God you are on the winning side, but God is calling you up higher as He did John on the Isle of Patmos:

> *After these things I looked, and behold, a door standing open in heaven. And the first voice which I heard was like a trumpet speaking with me, saying, "Come up here, and I will show you things which must take place after this."* (Revelation 4: 1).

John gets this call after he has seen the risen Lord in all His glory and has fallen flat on his face. John, the disciple to whom much revelation had already been given, is smitten and falls face down when he beholds His Majesty.

John has had an encounter with the King of Kings and Lord of Lords, and he will never be the same again; he will never live from the same place again. His eyes have seen the King in His Majesty, His beauty, and His power and this King indicates he wants John to see something.

Our journey is the same. At first we are captivated by His love; walking closely with Him; the lover of our souls; enjoying sweet fellowship. Then He calls us to come up higher and we see something of Him and His Majesty that we have never seen before. We fall face down in His Presence.

There is a higher place from which to live, He invites us now to come and partake of His nature, leaving our old self and our old ways behind us because He wants to show us something more.

Like the shrill of an alarm clock it wakes us from our slumber.

If we are living in our flesh, otherwise known as our lower nature, when He wants us living in the Spirit, the higher place, the higher nature. He calls us as He did the maiden in the Song of Songs:

> *"Rise up, my love, my fair one, and come away."* (Song of Songs 2:10).

He calls the maiden up to a high place where she can see the work of the evil one and understand her place in His plan for her life because she is no ordinary mortal. He has chosen her to be His eternal companion.

If you follow the narrative, you will see she falters and is slow in her responses to Him at first. Eventually He calls her again in chapter 4, first reassuring her that she is without spot in His eyes:

> *You are all fair, my love,*
> *And there is no spot in you.*
> *Come with me from Lebanon, my spouse,*
> *With me from Lebanon.*
> *Look from the top of Amana,*
> *From the top of Senir and Hermon,*
> *From the lions' dens,*
> *From the mountains of the leopards.*
> *"Come up to a high place", He calls, "come up higher,*
> *and higher still..."* (Song of Songs 4:7-8).

As we continue to study the Sermon on the Mount and the principles of conduct required of those who are to inherit the Kingdom and live life from the highest place, we will constantly be the call we will hear in our spirit: come up higher, high, higher, highest.

God want us *living* from the throne room, where He sits:

> *It is He who sits above the circle of the earth, and its inhabitants are like grasshoppers, who stretches out the heavens like a curtain, and spreads them out like a tent to dwell in.* (Isaiah 40:22).

His Majesty.

This is Him with whom we have to do. **This** is where we are meant to be living. **This** is where God has placed us in Jesus, in heavenly places in Christ.

If we are to reach for His highest, we need a dose of consummate reality.

We are in the army. Jesus is the Captain of the Host. The Sermon on the Mount is our operations manual. We have a task to perform and a purpose to fulfil.

Welcome (again) to boot camp.

High, higher, highest.

MEET THE AUTHOR

Beryl Moore is first and foremost: spiritually – a passionate lover of God and naturally – a mother and a grandmother.

Passionate about the Kingdom of God, as her lifestyle and teaching reflects, she believes every Christian can and should hear God for themselves.

She majors on teaching prophecy, spiritual warfare and leadership with an emphasis on the need to return to a God-centred lifestyle, by restoring the Creator/creature relationship to its proper place of honour, respect and intimacy.

Reading extensively, with an interest in the early church fathers and mystics such as Julian of Norwich, Madam Guyon, Teresa of Avila and Bernard of Clairveaux, and more recent prophets including A. W. Tozer and Graham Cooke, Beryl's work reflects her desire for the Kingdom to come in the lives of her audience.

Currently her main role involves raising up leaders, warriors and champions through training, consultancy and mentoring; with a particular emphasis on training leaders.

She lives in a small village in Kent where she works alongside the leader of a local church assisting in building a strong community of believers who focus on living a Kingdom lifestyle and bringing heaven to earth.

Originally called into the deliverance and healing ministry her focus changed ten years ago from 'hands-on' ministry to imparting knowledge to others. She is both eager and willing to share everything she knows to anyone who is interested.

With a love for God and His word, Beryl's philosophy is what she gently refers to as 'replacement theology' the renewal of our minds as we abide in the place Jesus died to give us, namely Himself. She teaches extensively on the need to abide, stay, dwell and remain where God the Father has placed us, in His Son. Her heart's desire is that all God's people know and experience the outrageous love of God.

For details of more of Beryl's teaching material, downloads and You Tube videos visit our website at www.sovereignministries. co.uk or www.psalm131.com

School of the Spirit

This is a not a book of theoretical principles but a route map for the journey that Beryl herself has taken into the heart of God. If you want 'more,' desire to 'go deeper,' and long to 'climb the mountain' with Jesus, then this will be your map, guide and handbook for the journey.

And don't race through, take your time to ponder, to chew, to listen to Father and Holy Spirit, and allow yourself to be changed forever. Fifty 'sessions' for you to encounter heaven on earth, to be transformed, and best of all, then help others to encounter Jesus more!

Thy Kingdom Come
Volume 2
'High, Higher, Highest'

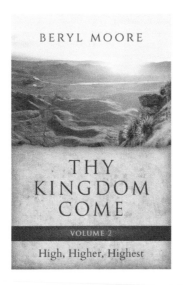

The second volume in this series is due for
release in Autumn 2020.